LOST, BUT NOT FOREVER

by

Mary Jane Warkentin

Feel a mother's heart-throb when her son was lost in the mountains.

Mary Jane Warkentin

© 2002 by Mary Jane Warkentin
All rights reserved.
No part of this book may be reproduced, stored in a retrieval system, or transmitted by any means, electronic, mechanical, photocopying, recording, or otherwise, without written permission from the author.

ISBN: 0-7596-3657-5

This book is printed on acid free paper.

1stBooks - rev. 05/10/02

Contents

PREFACE v
1. WHERE DID HE GO? 1
2. BOY ON A ROCK 12
3. TALKING TO THE AIRPLANES 21
4. THE CAMERAMAN LEFT TOO SOON 26
5. POSSES, ROCK CLIMBERS, AND A HELICOPTER 31
6. SCOTT'S FIELD OF FLOWERS 39
7. AT LAST A SIGN 48
8. THE BIBLE SAYS SO 54
9. YOU COULD FEEL THE POWER OF THE SPIRIT 61
10. A DOG NAMED GRACE 66
11. THERE'S AN EMPTINESS INSIDE 73
12. IT WAS LIKE A SANDWICH 79
13. JUST IN TIME FOR THE DRESS PARADE 87
14. EVERYONE HELPED HIS NEIGHBOR 95
15. MYSTERIOUS SURPRISES 100
16. A TREACHEROUS RAFT TRIP 106
17. MINE SEARCHING 111
18. NEVER ALONE 116
19. A TIME OF ANXIETY 121
20. AN UNUSUAL BOAT RIDE 129
21. A DOUBLE PORTION 134
22. TO GOD BE THE GLORY 137
23. HE HADN'T YET BEGUN 143
24. BITTERSWEET OBEDIENCE 151
25. CAMPING FUN 155
26. WHY? 157
27. MORE AND MORE 160
28. HOPELESS 164
29. NOTHING SPECIAL 169
EPILOGUE 171

PREFACE

I live near a freeway overpass, and I often have occasion to drive up there. Upon approaching the crest, instead of taking in a panoramic view of the city, my eyes always reach farther toward the beautiful, distant Sierra Nevada Mountains.

Usually it's a disappointment—I can't see the mountains at all because of the city smog!

But those hills are always there whether I can see them or not. It makes no difference what may come between me and the hills, for <u>they</u> never change. They are big, strong and majestic—they are there.

Yet, on a rare day the air will be clear—usually after a stormy time—and the lovely snow-laden sight will be more than worth the waiting! My first impression when I can see them is always the same: "Oh, how close they are!" In my mind, I always picture those gorgeous scenes as being farther away than they really are.

God, too, is always there whether I see Him or not, and He is closer than I had imagined him to be. Many ugly things in my life—like the smog—may hide the view and I may feel very alone. But He never changes! That is the moment when my faith begins to grow. He is there! He does care! Always! I need to keep looking up. I lift my eyes to Him for help, and His presence is with me during good times and bad. After a stormy time He will seem more near, and I will be glad to have trusted Him in the dark hour. When I was a student at Wheaton College, the president, Dr. V. Raymond Edmond, often said, "Never doubt in the dark what God told you in the light."

This is the true story of the search for our son who was lost in the mountains. My husband, Joel, and I lived through it—every anxious minute of it! Now that the worst is over, we both are convinced that God knows what He is doing whether we understand it or not. He is active in our lives, cares about our concerns, and can be trusted to do what is best! He was always there with us, but only occasionally could we see the evidence of His presence. Yet He did many things for us, including some that were quite amazing.

We want to share this whole fascinating story with you. What God did for us in coping with a frustrating situation, He can do for anyone.

Reach out and let Him touch and comfort you. He is always there, and is still a good God!

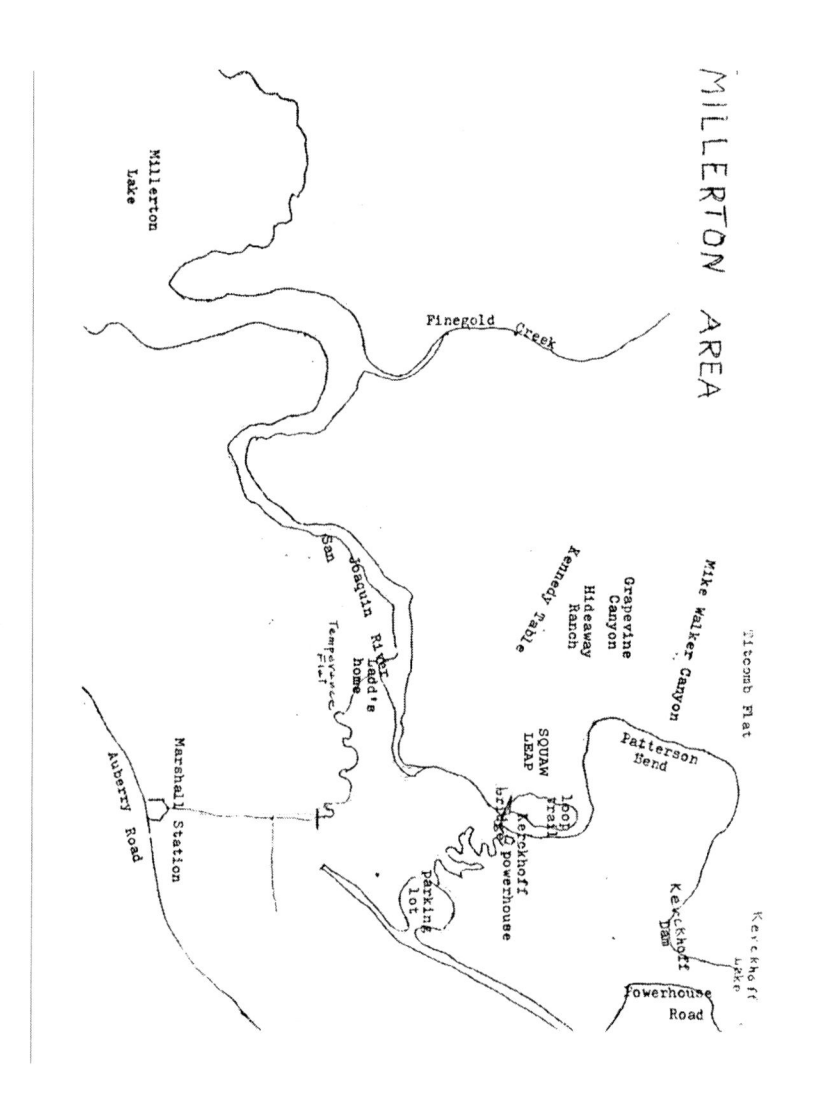

1

WHERE DID HE GO?

It was 4:00 A.M.

We were desperate!

As we sat in the car, my husband and I knew that our son had to be somewhere in the vast darkness of the surrounding mountains. A heavy, dull gloominess seemed to hang in the air, because Joel and I had no idea where Scott was. We did know that he had to be in deep trouble!

"Maybe he's caught in something," my husband said thinking aloud, "or he's injured, bitten by a snake, fallen into an old mine, drowned, been kidnapped—who knows what? We've got to find him!" Yes, Scott was a teenager and should have known what he was doing, but none of that made a bit of difference to us now, because he was gone, and we wanted him back!

It had all happened so innocently the afternoon before when Joel, Scott, and I drove up to a river area called Squaw Leap for a family picnic. We went just to enjoy the abundant bloom of wild flowers that were right now at their very prettiest.

The three of us had attended an early church service that morning. Scott sat between Joel and me in the pew. What a fine young man he was! I especially enjoyed listening to his newly-acquired deep bass voice, as he joined in singing God's praises, The worship service had put us all in a good mood. What a wonderful God! How close we felt to Him that day.

The forty-five-mile drive after church into the mountains from Fresno had been refreshing, for we loved viewing God's matchless handiwork. Scott had even excitedly spotted two deer darting up a hillside!

Perhaps it was a strange time for me to tell Scott how much I had wanted a fifth baby before he was born, but I had never mentioned this to him and now I wanted him to know. So, as we drove along, I mused aloud on how seemingly foolish it had been

Mary Jane Warkentin

Our son, Scott

Lost, But Not Forever

to wish for another child. I had told my mother one day that I wanted something very much.

"Is it anything I can give you?" she asked.

"No—it's a baby."

She turned white with shock! After recovering, she calmly remarked, "Oh, I wish you wouldn't bring another child into this world. It's such a wicked place!"

"But I wanted you anyway—so badly!" I told Scott as we rode along, ascending higher into the mountains. "And I was very happy when I found that you were on the way."

So this beautiful Sunday, after explaining all this to our son, I confronted him with a question: "Scott, are you glad that we brought you into the world anyway? Isn't it great to be alive?" I listened for his answer, but it must have been too embarrassing a question for a fifteen-year old boy.

When we arrived, and were spreading out our ground cloth for a picnic, a stranger walked up to us with the comment, "You'd better not sit here; there's going to be a lot of shooting."

"Shooting? Let's get out of here," I muttered, a bit stunned at the thought of such a thing going on in this magnificent sanctuary of nature. But I lingered to ask, "What are you planning to shoot?"

"Rifles," answered the unofficial-looking man. But with a smile he added, "Oh, it's just target practice. We have a large group of riflemen, and it won't be safe for you on this side of the road. Are you going to have a picnic?" He scanned the contents of our hurriedly-prepared cardboard box.

"We wanted to."

"Well, just go over there anywhere, because we don't want anyone getting hurt," he told us, motioning. "I'm sure that'll be all right."

Picking up our things, we moved across the road and a little further down. "How's this?" Joel asked, as he stepped into a fresh flower-strewn meadow.

"O.K," I said a bit skeptically, as I cast a glance around to be sure we were a safe distance from the shooters. A bullet can go a long way, I reasoned. So again we spread out the patchwork ground cloth that I had sewn together from the pant legs of many worn-out jeans. We laid it carefully over the lush grass and flowers.

After two seasons of drought in California and many prayers for rain, this year had been very different—it had rained and rained all winter! Now it was April, and as we surveyed the scene in all directions, there was nowhere to walk without stepping on a flower.

We had first heard of Squaw Leap the day before from the newspaper. A hundred or so others probably read the article and had come to enjoy its beauties on such a lovely afternoon. Usually it was a much more forsaken area—not a very well-known spot for an outing.

"O.K., let's go to it!" Joel blurted. Mechanically I'd been laying out the food from our big box. We always kept a picnic simple. Joel seemed to like it that way—throw a few things together and enjoy it as if it were a royal banquet. What a happy time it was—just the three of us! We tried to ignore the constant sound of rifles firing not too far away.

Eating completed, Scott asked expectantly, "Are we going on a hike?" There was nothing he enjoyed more than a good hike, and the wilder spot the better. Our son was a real nature-lover, often stooping to examine and admire a single plant along the way.

"We'll take the path down to the river," Joel had already decided. "It's about a mile down. There's supposed to be a bridge over the San Joaquin River when you reach the bottom."

I always needed a nap after lunch. I'd hoped they would wait for me, but, a little disappointed, I told them to go on ahead. "I'll join you later," I explained. I could see they were anxious to get started.

Lost, But Not Forever

The two started toward the trail. At six feet two, Joel towered only slightly above long, lanky Scott. Our boy had shot up so fast we hardly knew him.

My husband and I had been married twenty-eight years. Rearing five children hadn't always been easy. Just two months earlier, the house had been full of youthful activity. Besides our four sons, a friend of theirs also stayed with us for a time, bedding down in the living room. But despite the hassles, I had been in my glory having them all around, tending to their needs. We all had great Christian fellowship together! Just recently two of the sons, Wayne and Ralph, had moved into apartments of their own. Now only Scott—the youngest—and twenty-three-year-old Donald lived at home. One daughter, Renetta, was married with a baby of her own.

Joel and Scott were out of sight now, so I packed up the remains of our meal and headed for the red station wagon, where a fluffy pillow was waiting. Although target practice was well underway, I was able to grab a quick refreshing snooze and was soon on my way toward the trail. What a pretty walk down the well-marked path! People of all ages—mostly in families—passed by, and usually a few words were exchanged with these friendly nature-loving folks.

A worshipful experience it was—revelling in the wisdom, power, and love of God Who had created these wonders! Miniature waterfalls trickled here and there. The path curved in crazy ways as it dipped lower toward the river. I felt ecstatic. Everything was unusually lush and vividly green. No hills had ever been more colorfully arrayed.

"Is it much farther to the river?" I asked a returning hiker as we passed.

"Oh, no, just around the next bend." My step quickened in anticipation, although I knew that I would never be able to catch up with Joel and Scott. Perhaps we'd meet on the way back. I could enjoy my own company anyway—and God's. He was so near.

Mary Jane Warkentin

"There it is," I said to myself, as the river and bridge came into view. What a delightful surprise to see Joel sitting on a rock across the river bridge! He had waited for me after all.

Together we admired the bridge, which spanned a granite gorge. The structure itself was supported by two massive steel arches. Between the arches, a walkway about ten feet wide had been built for humans and horse traffic. The deck was about twenty-five feet above the ice-cold, churning San Joaquin River, which was full of whirlpools and rapids. A large powerhouse stood nearby. A picture of the bridge on the cover of this book was taken by my husband just before I arrived that day.

Scott

Lost, But Not Forever

"Where's Scott?" I questioned my husband as we exchanged smiles.

"He's gone up the trail to see what's ahead," was his simple reply. "I stayed behind to take a few pictures." Then he added excitedly, "Mary Jane, you must go with me! I came back to get you because the trail on the other side of the river is even more beautiful than the one you've just seen! Come and I'll show you." We began to follow the path that led beyond the river. He was right. It was breathtaking beyond imagination— a veritable fairyland! Arm in arm we strolled, marveling at each new colorful vista.

We didn't dare go too far, since we absolutely had to be home again in time to attend our son, Donald's, concert that evening. So we soon headed back, the sounds of the rifle fire still reverberating in our ears.

Scott might pass us on the trail, I thought, or more likely he would be waiting at the parking lot. He enjoyed taking his own little side trips on family outings, and had done so on numerous occasions. We seldom had to wait, since he was an excellent judge of time.

The cool air was invigorating, and we arrived at the parking lot sooner than we had expected. Scott was not there, so we decided to relax on the grass at the head of the trail and watch the people come and go. There was less reason to rush now.

Donald's concert would top off this already pleasant day. How we had all looked forward to this evening! Now a university graduate, he enjoyed singing and was a bass in a five-hundred-voice choir. We couldn't wait to see our son perform!

But why didn't Scott come? We hoped he wouldn't make us late for the choir concert.

"Did you see that map of the trails?" asked Joel, passing the time.

"No."

"Let's go look at it. The path where we started to walk from the bridge on the other side of the river turns into a big loop-shaped trail." We walked a short distance to a large wooden sign that sketched all the trails and other features of the area. As we studied the map, a striking thought seemed to hit both of us.

I spoke first. "How big is the Loop?"

We looked at the sign, but it didn't give this information. "If Scott began walking around that loop, not knowing how far it was, he could be gone a long time!"

"You're right," agreed Joel. "And that was just the way he was headed. He always likes to go to the end of the trail." We were both beginning to get impatient.

"What's he trying to do—walk around that whole loop?" I fretted. "He can't do that and be back here in time! Doesn't he know that?" Joel shrugged his shoulders.

We watched the people as they emerged from the trail. The sun was sinking lower. Fewer and fewer hikers were returning. Angry thoughts ran through my mind. Next time we'll leave Scott at home and go by ourselves if he can't get back here! It was past time to leave and we'd be lucky now to hear even part of the concert. "Why doesn't he come?" I thought.

"Joel," I finally asked softly. "could he be lost?" Little knots of fear were forming in my stomach.

"I don't know, my dear." Our eyes met and we gazed in outward calmness.

I had to do something. "I'm going to the head of the trail and talk to the people coming up," I suggested.

"Go ahead—whatever you think might help."

A bit stiff from sitting so long, I awkwardly made it up and headed toward the trail, where a few stragglers were still returning from the river area.

"Hello," I ventured to say to one couple. "Did you by any chance see a fifteen-year-old blond boy by himself down there anywhere? He's six feet tall and very slender."

"No, we didn't," but their eyes were kind.

A young man with a backpack was heading down the trail even at this late hour. He would be a good one to tell. "Say, if you're going down the trail toward the river, would you mind keeping your eyes open for our son?" I asked hopefully. "He's

Lost, But Not Forever

fifteen, very tall and slim, wearing a tan shirt and tan polyester pants. He ought to be back by now—unless he's lost." My voice dropped.

"Sure will." He had such confidence. "I'm going all the way to the lake, so I'll watch for him."

I began asking everyone I saw! No one had even seen our son. It was already beginning to get dark. We had to find him! He must be going clear around that loop, I thought, and who knows how far that is? He was by now an hour and a half late. How could Scott do this to us?

"Joel," I began, "it's too bad the map doesn't give distances. We have no idea how far the loop trail is, or how long it might take to hike around it; it could mean anything from half an hour to all night! Scott could walk and walk, always thinking he is getting back to the bridge and yet actually going farther away all the time. It's messed us all up! We've already missed the whole concert. But...maybe he's not on the loop. He could be really lost!"

The two of us were utterly bewildered.

"Should we call the sheriff?" Joel asked, glancing at his watch for the umpteenth time. Mine said it was already past six o'clock.

I checked around in every direction. "Call from where?" I felt helpless. "There's no phone here. Where's the nearest telephone?"

"Probably in Auberry; that's about seven miles."

"Would they do anything if you did report it?" I was skeptical.

"Probably not until morning now. It isn't freezing tonight, and they'd say, 'He will be okay until we can get at it tomorrow.'"

"Well, I think we'd better call him anyway."

Joel hesitated a bit, then thoughtfully answered, "I would have to drive all the way to Auberry."

"And take the station wagon?" I balked at the thought. "What will Scott do when he gets back to the parking lot and finds nothing here? Then he may take off down the road and we'll never find him."

Why hadn't I thought of it?— "I'm going to 'trill'."

I might have lost all my children many times if it hadn't been for the "trill". I'd learned it from my mother years ago, who had called all her children that way. The dog always thought it was meant for her, too. Our offspring always came the minute they heard it.

"Trrrrh," I sounded.

Then louder— "TRRRRRH!" I trilled as loudly as I could, but this time it didn't bring results. Scott did not come.

"Would you stay here in case Scott shows up while I go phone the sheriff?" Joel questioned.

"I guess I could. I'll have to. But it's almost dark and I'll be all alone here. And it's getting so cold!"

"Then I'll stay and you do the phoning."

That was worse. "I wouldn't know where to go and I'd get lost for sure. I wish we could stay together. Oh, if there were just a telephone around here! What about those houses alongside the road on the way up? Maybe…"

"Mary Jane! Look, a sheriff's car!" Sure enough, there was a deputy sheriff driving right into the deserted parking lot where we were standing. We couldn't believe our eyes.

Lost, But Not Forever

Scott Warkentin

2

BOY ON A ROCK

We both ran quickly to the officer's car.

"I have a report of a boy stranded on a rock down by the river bridge," the deputy sheriff began without delay. "I got the call in Auberry. On the way over here two or three cars stopped to inform me of the incident." The deputy told us that a ten-foot rope had been let down to the lad, but it had not been long enough.

We brightened up. "It must be our son," Joel said. "He's lost down there somewhere."

"Yes," I added, "that's just like Scott to get stuck on a rock and not be able to get off." Poor kid, down there all this time by himself! It was a relief to think that someone had at least seen him. He must be expecting to spend the night now on the hard, cold rock.

Thank you, God, for bringing this sheriff to us, we both thought.

"I'm new in this area," the deputy admitted. "Can I get through to the river by that road?" He motioned toward the target practice area.

"We've never been here before ourselves," replied Joel, "but I'm quite sure there's no way down to the river but by the foot path."

I was relieved that this deputy wasn't going to wait until morning! He went right into action and immediately called for a deputy to come with a long rope. "I'll drive up here, just to see where this road goes. You stay and tell the other deputy where I am when he comes," the man ordered hurriedly.

"I think there is a road to the powerhouse on the other side of the parking lot," said Joel.

"I'll check that out too." The deputy, whose name was Bill, was off. The first road ended a short distance beyond its starting

Lost, But Not Forever

point, and the way to the powerhouse was locked securely with a chain. The deputy returned and radioed for someone to try to locate the key. Then he said to Joel, "Come on, let's hike down to the bridge and see what we can find."

"You stay here in the car," Joel said to me, then tenderly kissed me. He and Bill started the mile-long hike to the river bridge, this time not just for fun.

It was hard for me to believe that someone else was seriously helping us to find our boy. I would have expected a lost son to be our own problem to figure out pretty much by ourselves.

I was shivering, and the warmth of the car felt good. Locking the doors for safety, I sat and watched them walk away in the twilight, then settled back into a comfortable position to wait.

"What will Scott do next?" I reflected. "He loves to climb around on rocks. If I were stuck on one, Scott would laugh while I struggled to get my big hulk moving again. But I've never really known that to happen to Scott. He is a fairly nimble fellow; but there always has to be a first time. My, isn't it amazing that the deputy sheriff drove right up to us when we needed him?"

Quietly I thanked the Lord. I was sure the men would find Scott now. But, what if they didn't? My head reeled at the thought and I quickly dismissed it. Surely it's just a matter of time. These men know what they're doing. It is good to know that God is always with us, no matter what happens.

A long time passed and I began to wander if they would ever return. They must be having a hard time with the boy on the rock. It's so dark outside! Oh, what a day this has been.

Suddenly a bright light shone toward the car, and I sat up quickly. It was the other deputy with the rope. "This is great," I told myself, "the way they're treating us! It's a shame to put the authorities to all this bother, but how grateful I am. We must have our boy back, and they seem determined to get him to us." I went outside.

Mary Jane Warkentin

This deputy introduced himself as Jerry. He had a good, strong rope, but even so, he was worried that it might not be long enough. However, he had a big flashlight that was extra bright. Jerry headed down the path to join Joel and the other deputy, who were now at the bridge.

"I don't find anyone down here," Bill announced to Joel. "You stay at the bridge as a sentry and I'll search the river banks." He disappeared quickly into the night, the shimmer of his flashlight slowly dimming until it was out of sight.

Joel looked at the bright stars and thought of God and His wonders. My, they were bright out tonight! Surely Scott would turn up somewhere, somehow. On the other hand, the roaring of the river affirmed the seriousness of the situation. The best swimmer could never cope with the turbulence of that current. Had something happened to Scott that claimed his life? A note of praise and confidence in God filled Joel's heart amid the half-fear that permeated the moments. The stars were a point of contact with the Creator Who was in control of the situation.

While Joel was on the bridge waiting for Bill's return, Jerry arrived with the rope and an extra flashlight.

"This place is snake heaven," Jerry said. He explained that fishermen wouldn't come there in the summertime because of the many rattlesnakes. It was now early April, so the reptiles had not yet come out of hibernation. According to the old-timers, large groups of snakes congregate for the winter, sleeping in a tight coil and emit a horrible stench when all packed together like this.

I was trying my best to be patient in the car. Probably Scott is terribly scared to hang on to the rope, I kept imagining, not blaming him for that. They really must be having a time with him! I glanced at my watch; it had been two hours since Joel left me.

Footsteps. I pricked up my ears to listen... finally! Their voices were barely audible. What a sight for sore eyes that kid

Lost, But Not Forever

will be! Should I kiss. him or bawl him out? Or both? He must be tired and shivering—how glad he'll be to get back home. We sure never imagined all this when we left home this morning! I wondered what they'd have to say.

I lowered the window. A deputy stepped up to the car with Joel beside him and calmly told me, "Mrs. Warkentin, we can't find your son anywhere."

My heart suddenly plummeted to the bottom of my feet and an electric shock seemed to run through my chilled body.

"I'm sorry, Ma'am," the deputy was saying. "There was no boy down there on a rock, and we don't know where your son is. I will radio at once for a search-and-rescue expert and his team from Shaver Lake. We will go out and hunt until we find him, if it takes all night." A gripping fear threatened to choke me; however, I was comforted some by the way these deputies were handling the situation.

Just then two headlights appeared from the opposite direction. I had noticed a pick-up go by before, and now it was coming back. Jerry commented, "Maybe he will have your boy!" We flagged the vehicle down and all walked over to it. The driver was alone.

"Have you seen a boy alongside the road anywhere?" one of the officers asked the man. "There is a teen-ager lost in this area." He had not seen anyone, but introduced himself as a hunter well acquainted with the vicinity and volunteered to help search for Scott.

After making a radio call for the expert searchers, the deputies and the hunter looked along the road and discussed with Joel what might have happened and possible things to do. I followed along in a daze. I felt myself to be sure I was really there—it could be just a dream. If so, I wished I'd wake up.

At ten o'clock Deputy Sheriff Artie Cox, the man in charge, arrived with two other search-and-rescue team members and professional equipment. The five deputies, along with the hunter, planned their strategy for the night.

"What shall I do to help?" inquired Joel.

Mary Jane Warkentin

"The best thing for you to do is stay with your wife. These men are experts and it is best if we leave it to them. Mary Jane will need you to be with her tonight." It was plain to see that Artie Cox was a diplomatic, tactful man who gave direct information in a courteous way.

Joel explained to him that our married daughter, Renetta, lived in the same hills—only seventeen miles away. We gave him her telephone number and suggested that we might go there to spend the night. The men left for an all-out search of the river area.

"Should we go to Renetta's?" Joel questioned.

I hunted for an answer. "I don't think so," I soon decided. "We can't take the car away from here. Scott may find his way back in the night. We'd better stay right here, don't you suppose?"

Joel agreed.

As we settled in, the hunter's dog began to bark. He wanted to go along with his master, but had been left chained to the pick-up on the other side of the parking lot. He howled and whined; my, how he yelped!

The cool night air and the eerie circumstances caused goose bumps on my arms. I glanced into the back seat to see what coat Scott had taken with him. Since the weather had been unpredictable, we had each brought along a light and a heavy coat. His light coat was still there—that was a relief. He had taken his heavily lined coat, but still I knew that wouldn't be enough. He could be cold down along the river in spite of it, for Scott always chilled easily. Even at fifteen, I always saw to it that Scott wore warm clothes at night, especially when we went camping. I would check that his sleeping bag was zipped up and his shoulders covered. Now I couldn't do anything about it. I felt so helpless! I wanted to reach out to him, but I didn't even know where he was, or if he was all right. The pain was real, and it grabbed me intensely in the pit of my stomach.

"What happened when you were down there?" I asked my husband at last. "Did you look everywhere? Wasn't there any

Lost, But Not Forever

boy on a rock?" Concealing my concern was out of the question. The uncertainty was agonizing.

"We couldn't find a soul," Joel answered, his voice strained. "Both deputies went a long way and looked all over. In fact, Jerry became concerned about Bill's being off by himself downstream because they always stay in pairs on a search. Jerry whistled for Bill to come back to the bridge. Bill had found no trace of a boy on a rock. Jerry shone his powerful light all around, Mary Jane."

"Well, let's pray about it together," I suggested, mustering up courage. Joel was hurting too. Christ had always been the center of our home and of our interests. What do husbands and wives do when they confront a crisis? We did as we'd long been accustomed to doing—we prayed. Softly each of us in turn spoke to our heavenly Father aloud, committing the whole predicament to Him.

I found a blanket in the back of the car and wrapped it around me. It felt good.

"One thing we must decide right now," Joel remarked firmly when we were settled again. "We will not blame ourselves." We both knew this could be devastating to our mental state. Besides, it could do no possible good. Joel was an easygoing type of person who generally took things as they came. He was not easily upset and didn't believe in worrying. "Never trouble Trouble until Trouble troubles you, for you'll only make your trouble Double-Trouble if you do," he often said. I always tried to remember that. This situation was proving to be a real test for even Joel's stability.

The dog continued to howl as we sat there.

"Would you like to say some Bible verses?" Joel asked. We usually read the Bible together, discussed it a little, and then prayed each evening. Sometimes we would simply quote verses. Surely we needed all the help we could get about now!

"Trust in the Lord with all thine heart," I began, "and lean not unto thine own understanding. In all thy ways acknowledge Him, and He shall direct thy paths" (Proverbs 3:5-6). The week

Mary Jane Warkentin

before in Sunday School, our class had been studying the book of Proverbs. The teacher had asked each one to share a favorite proverb, and this was the one we both had chosen.

"Now we have an opportunity to put our faith into action and experience the truths of those verses."

"We surely do!" I agreed. "He shall direct thy paths"—that was the important part. "Oh, direct the paths of the deputies out there!" I murmured. "O Lord, direct their paths to where Scott is." We quoted a few other helpful scriptures to each other. There was tremendous comfort in reflecting on God's Word.

The dog was still yanking on his chain and yelping. I felt sorry for him. We knew he wasn't going to quiet down until his owner returned. Nevertheless, because it was late, we decided to try to get some sleep, We bundled up as best we could and settled down in the front seat. The two pillows that I'd thrown in for my nap came in handy. Joel was good at snoozing sitting up, so I put my pillow in his lap. Prayers for God's help continued to pour from our hearts.

Clang! The dog had broken the chain and was off into the blackness of the night. Now all was quiet. He had finally managed to work himself loose somehow.

Both of us had short spurts of sleep after that. It was amazing that we could rest, but it says God "giveth His beloved sleep" (Psalm 127:2).

We were still God's dear children and so was our missing son, wherever he was. In spite of outward circimstances, God had not forsaken us. We each had committed our lives to Christ in our youthful days, and we had trusted Him for many years. We often voiced our faith and taught Bible truths to others, but was this faith real? Could it stand up now, even with our boy down there somewhere in this wild, remote region? God's gracious love was with us.

"God, You know where Scott is! Take care of him. God..." I fell asleep calling out to the God Whom the Bible says never slumbers or sleeps.

Lost, But Not Forever

I awoke with a start, and looked around. Everything was the same; the deputies had not come back. Nobody had found Scott! I flicked on the dome light, and saw that it was almost three o'clock in the middle of the night. Scott—where was he? He was out there in the cold! Oh, it was cold!

I couldn't stand such an irksome predicament!!

Suddenly I began to feel all closed in, and fiery hot. Panic struck me. I tore off my heavy coat, then the inner one. I felt compelled to fling open the car door; frigid air rushed in. It was an awful moment! I felt these deep sobs coming out of me like those of a wounded animal, as tears began pouring down my face.

Joel sensed something and woke up. "Can I do anything for you, dear?" he asked gently.

"I can't take this—" I yelled, "having Scott wandering around out there! I just can't stand it!"

"I know," he answered.

Had God forsaken us? We felt so alone and confused. Finally I was able to cool off and settle down again, and was even blessed with another snooze.

At four A.M. Artie Cox returned to the parking lot and stepped over to our car. Immediately we both were aware of his presence and woke with a start. Joel thrust open the door. Would he know anything? Or would it just be another disappointment? The searchers would have to know something definite by now!

"We have circled the complete loop and searched for footprints all around, and we find nothing helpful at all," he reported.

This time it was as though a dagger suddenly struck me and was left quivering in my chest. This was unbelievable. I felt numb all over. What a situation! Now what? Where could he possibly be after all this time? Oh, God, where are You?

Artie continued, "I'll head off now and arrange for a couple of airplanes to be over the area as soon as the sun comes up. We've got excellent fliers here that you can't beat."

Mary Jane Warkentin

"Boy, that sure is a good idea!" I thought, encouraged.

Then he said, "I'm absolutely soaked."

Amazed, I looked up. "Oh, you mean with sweat?" I realized that even in the closed car it was quite chilly, and out there it surely was much more so; yet this man, who didn't even know our son, had literally poured himself out for us all night.

"And I'm bushed," he added. We felt a certain awe in the presence of such dedication. There was still goodness left in this world.

"At least you can go home now and get some much needed rest," I said. I had to find something to be glad about.

"I'll get a few winks," Artie responded. "I have to shower right away to wash off all this poison oak; it's full of it down there, you know. I'll be back here at eight o'clock to oversee operations."

He said it all so casually. Someone was going all out to help us in our dilemma. Our appreciation in return seemed so shallow. Mere words were insufficient.

3

TALKING TO THE AIRPLANES

It was a little after 4 A.M. when the search team left. Once again Joel and I decided to try to get a little rest. We needed to be ready for whatever this new day would bring. It was like a bad dream, trying to wake up and you can't.

As I lay there, I caught myself thinking, "The Bible says, 'One day is with the Lord as a thousand years' (2 Peter 3:8). I wouldn't want a thousand years of this kind of day!" Again my mind went to prayer. There was no deciding, "Shall I pray, or shall I not?" There burst forth an automatic stream of prayer reaching up to Almighty God, asking for help. In a way, I wanted to put my entire trust in Artie and the airplanes, but I knew I had to look higher. "My help cometh from the Lord, which made heaven and earth" (Psalm 121: 2), I quoted to myself.

I tried shifting my position. Joel and I were still cramped into the front seat of the car because of the cold. I was restless, and something more comfortable didn't seem possible.

Suddenly it dawned upon me that right now no one was even looking for Scott! He was there, wherever he was, all alone! Was he still walking, hoping to find his way? Had he finally given up and lay down, and was trying to sleep? At the same instant I wondered if he would freeze if he did! No, I decided with relief, the temperature wasn't that cold. But he must be shivering to death! Why wasn't he found on that rock? Was that some other boy? It surely would help if we knew whether or not that boy was Scott. "Oh God, take care of our Scott. You know where he is—the very spot. We trust You to help us. Thank You for the airplanes that are coming. Use them. Oh, Jesus, help them." The torment of not knowing was painful, yet I was sure that God knew all about it, and that He still loved all of us very much.

An airplane flew overhead—and then passed on. Another, but it went right by. It was almost 7 A.M. and we got up and stood in the parking lot watching for planes. The sun was already very bright. I wished they'd get at it! Artie had said the airplanes would be at Squaw Leap first thing in the morning. They should be here soon!

"I'd better go and find a telephone somewhere," Joel told me. "I need to call the high school to let them know I won't be teaching today." Joel had always been a hard worker, and a faithful provider for the family. He taught government classes and then even moonlighted teaching driver training. "I'll call Renetta, too," he added, "and the boys, to let them know what's happening."

The empty parking lot seemed very desolate after Joel left. I walked aimlessly, thinking of how crowded this place had been just the day before. How happy and relaxed everyone had been! Now it all looked so serene. The flowers were as pretty as ever, but somehow they took on a different hue. All was quiet except for a few birds that twittered here and there, innocently unaware of our crisis. It almost seemed as if we could forget it all and go home. My thoughts raced wildly. "Surely Scott has to be at home in bed, sleeping late because he didn't hear the alarm go off. He needs me to go wake him. No, he should be at school by now. But he isn't!" I had to tell myself, "He's here...hidden from everyone's view behind a bush...snoozing between the rocks...walking...looking...bewildered...lonesome...longing to find us, too." It dazzled my mind.

Getting through to our other children—Wayne, Renetta, Donald, and Ralph—was not an easy task for Joel. The sheriffs had to help us. The authorities finally had to visit our home to rouse Donald and to check out the possibility that Scott had somehow found his way home. They also phoned to see if he might have caught a ride to our daugther's house. Immediately Renetta pulled the baby out of his comfy bed and, with her husband Rick, and his father, sped along the hilly roads to Joel's side at Squaw Leap. Joel quickly cued everyone in on the

Lost, But Not Forever

essential details, then he and his son-in-law set out for the bridge to check out the Loop Trail for themselves. Renetta, the baby, and Rick's father, Bud, stayed with me in the parking lot.

Our son, Ralph, had reported for work on Monday morning flashing his usual big, winning smile, but his boss had greeted him with a very serious look of surprise. "I didn't think you'd come today," he said. "Did they find Scott?" Ralph had not heard a thing, but his boss had seen the news in the morning paper.

His brother, Wayne, found out about it in a similar way. He had happened to stop by our house to pick up his mail, when the phone rang. It was Joel's sister. She had heard the news and wanted to know if Scott had been found.

Both boys had recently moved out of our house and had no telephones yet, so it had been impossible for anyone to reach them from the parking lot. Finally they were able to contact one another. Wayne picked up Ralph, and they headed for the hills in a state of bewilderment.

As Joel and Rick approached the bridge, a strange-looking human-like form was spotted in the river. Joel was filled with horror as the thought struck him that it could be Scott's body. "Oh no, Lord, don't let it be!" Joel pleaded. Rick had his field glasses with him, and examined the form. It was only a moss-covered rock.

When they came to the loop, they realized that probably very few people had walked that way since Scott disappeared. Artie had said the footprints that were there were not helpful. Nevertheless Rick decided to memorize the design of each tennis shoe sole print, just in case. There were only five different patterns near Scott's size on the Loop Trail. He was determined to make something of it.

"It would help if I knew exactly what Scott's shoe soles looked like," he thought, "but I guess there's really no way to know."

Later Rick talked with me about it. "Sure," I answered, "we have two pairs of tennis shoes just like that in our family."

"You do?" Rick was surprised.

"Yes, Joel bought them when they were on sale. So 'just in case' he purchased two pairs—figuring with four boys in the family, they'd come in handy. It's the only time we ever bought two shoes alike at the same time." The other pair was still at home unworn.

"Hey, that's great!" shouted Rick, much encouraged. "This will really help us."

It did, at least, give us a much needed morale booster.

A little after 8 A.M. Artie Cox arrived.

"Did you get your few winks?" I inquired, feeling sorry for him, being up all night tramping around that rough terrain, and now here again the next morning. Yet I was enormously grateful for his presence.

"Not many winks," Artie answered. "But it will have to do. That's often the way it is on a search." He took things so calmly. We felt confident that he was just the man for the job. "The airplanes should be here soon," he told us all with anticipation.

It was hard to wait and my mind began wandering again. "What in the world really did happen to Scott?" I asked myself. "He has to be somewhere! Maybe a rattlesnake bit him and he is lying there with his leg all puffed up. Did he fall? He may have a broken leg. He could even be unconscious. Surely he'd be back from the Loop Trail by this time no matter how long it was—unless he couldn't find us again! Would there be wild animals out there? Maybe he got kidnapped. Surely he hasn't drowned in the river. Our family was always so careful around water. Well, the airplanes will spot him wherever he is— if they ever get here! God, please help them to find our boy."

The sound of engines broke the silence. A Cessna 140 came into sight—then another. That roar was the real thing!

"These pilots are volunteers," Artie explained as the airplanes approached. "They are expert flyers: you couldn't ask for any better men. One will be flying along the river, and the other will circle higher up to watch and advise him if anything goes wrong because it is very dangerous."

"Take good care of them, Lord," my prayer went up from the parking lot. Joel, too, was praying on the trail, "Please, Lord, protect that pilot! I don't want anyone killed looking for Scott." As they hiked the Loop Trail, Rick and Joel could see the pilot in his cabin. Of course the pilot spotted them too, and they waved to each other. The lower of the two planes was just missing the treetops. It went up the river on one side, circling around and down, then flew up the other side, turned and went downstream again, criss-crossing the river gorge, then pulling into a steep climb as the pilot approached the ridge.

In the parking lot everyone stood around Artie's car. A voice radioed intermittently.

"That talking is from our plane," Artie informed the group. "We have a direct communication system." He told the pilots in the planes, "Those two men down there are searchers; one is the father."

"Have the pilots seen anything?" I finally ventured impatiently.

"Not yet." Artie's voice was reassuring. "Wait a minute. The lower plane has observed something brown on a rock." My heart jumped; Scott had been wearing tan clothes!

"He will have to make another round to see it again," Artie said. "I'll tell him when he reaches the spot."

It seemed like an eternity...but finally Artie informed the pilot, "The place is under you right...NOW!" Yes, the pilot saw it, too, but he couldn't tell what it was. Artie had to send someone to walk down and investigate.

About an hour later we found out that the brown "something" was only an old, rusty, oil barrel.

4

THE CAMERAMAN LEFT TOO SOON

I had a suggestion. "Could you bring dogs in to try to find Scott? He may be injured or caught down under something where the airplanes can't see him." I thought it was a great idea.

"We've never had great success with dogs; there's really no use in trying that," was Artie's answer. My spirits suddenly plummeted to the ground.

Rick's father, Bud, was also asking questions and doing a lot of pondering. Finally he said thoughtfully, "If I were you, Mary Jane, I'd go down to the valley and get on television."

"Me? On television?" I spurted out. "But my hair's a mess."

"What difference does that make?" said Bud. "Besides, it's O.K. The best thing you could do for all of us right now would be to put a call for the 'boy on the rock' to identify himself. And that means getting on T.V. Someone may have seen him and can tell us more about what happened down there. It just might be the key to this mystery." The idea sounded very convincing and sensible, but not too appealing to me.

I began imagining myself on the television screen. Surely if I did that, I'd want to spend all morning in the beauty parlor to make myself presentable. And I'd don my prettiest dress. I glanced down at my wrinkled blouse that I had slept (?) in all night. "I have to wear this?" I thought in disgust. I knew I'd never get to stop by the house so I could change, and now I was stuck with what I had on. It would have looked fine yesterday—at least passable, but now? My face felt haggard, but how should a mother be when her boy is lost in the mountains? I was sure I looked the part. "What does that matter anyway?" I realized, suddenly feeling ashamed for even thinking of myself at a time like this.

Lost, But Not Forever

"How will I get there?" I still hated to take the car away, in case Scott needed it.

"I'll take you," Bud quickly offered, "and right now if you like."

It didn't seem that the airplanes were making any great discoveries, although they were continuing to fly painstakingly back and forth. I might as well try TV.

When I mentioned the thought to Artie, he was ready with instructions. "Call the sheriff's office and ask for Chet. Tell him what you want to do, and ask him to get permission from Channel 47. I'm sure they will put you on."

It all seemed settled. Then I thought it over to be sure that I wanted to leave my daughter, grandson, and the airplanes in the mountains. Yes, it was for the best. Maybe some important information would be revealed.

"O.K., let's go. I'm as ready as I'll ever be."

"Great! Get in," called Bud, and the truck was soon rattling down the bumpy mountain roads.

"I'd better decide what I'm going to say." Taking an old shopping list out of my purse, I began to formulate my thoughts and to jot them down as best I could in the swaying truck.

> Our son has disappeared near the San Joaquin River above Millerton Lake in the Squaw Leap area. A report Sunday afternoon told of a boy stuck on a rock by the bridge. If anyone knows anything about this boy—who he was, his possible age, the location of the rock, or any information—please don't hesitate to call the Sheriff's Department. It could be very helpful to us.

That accomplished, I said. "Would you mind, Bud, if I put my head down? I'm really very tired."

"I understand."

As Bud and I rode along in silence, my thoughts seemed as loud as words: "Will Scott be found today?" I wondered as a persistent ache welled up in my stomach. "He must be getting

Mary Jane Warkentin

hungry! At least the sun is out now, and it's not so chilly out there. Likely he was up most of the night, but by now he may be curled up somewhere. Yes, he's probably been sleeping all morning, and that's why the airplanes can't see him! Maybe by noon he will be up and they can spot him—if they'll just stick with it that long! "You help them find Scott, dear Lord! He's Your child, too. You love him, don't you? I know You want him to be found. Oh, God, where is he? Please, God. Scott loves You, too. Please help us!" How I ached, wanting to pick him out of the air somewhere and throw my arms around him. But he was always beyond my reach.

No doubt Scott was doing a lot of praying himself! I was sure he must be. He knew how. All of the children prayed aloud whenever we had family devotions. Someone had said that the best way to raise children was to pray for them and to pray with them. Although Scott's prayers sometimes sounded immature or mechanical, still I knew that he had a genuine relationship with God. He was hesitant to reveal his inner feelings to us, but I was quite sure that he really did open up his heart when he was alone with God. Our son was always glad to go to church, and the few times we left him at home alone—when we were out of town—he would ride his bike, walk, or do anything to be in God's House on Sundays. "He probably feels closer to God now in this crisis than he ever has in his life," I told myself.

Even though I was tired, I felt God's presence all about me. I comforted myself with the thought of some Bible verses: "Who shall separate us from the love of Christ? shall tribulation, or distress, or persecution, or famine, or nakedness, or peril, or sword?...Nay, in all these things we are more than conquerors through him that loved us. For I am persuaded that neither death, nor life, nor angels, nor principalities, nor powers, nor things present, nor things to come, nor height, nor depth, nor any other creature, shall be able to separate us from the love of God, which is in Christ Jesus our Lord" (Romans 8: 35, 37-39). How glad I was that I had memorized all that during another difficult time of my life when I was younger!

Lost, But Not Forever

"How's this?" Bud interrupted my thoughts. I looked up as he stopped the pickup.

"Where are we?" I asked.

"We're in town. There's a phone booth here. Get any rest?"

"Yes, I feel better. I'll call the T.V. station from here." I began to feel a little scared that I might do something wrong!

The pay telephone was outdoors and close to four lanes of noisy traffic. I hoped I'd be able to hear myself think! After dialing the number that Artie had given me, Chet answered the phone. I explained my mission.

"You stay there while I make arrangements, and I'll call you right back," he advised.

It was a hot place to wait, with an endless stream of cars pouring exhaust into our faces. When other people came to use the phone, we had to explain that we were expecting a very important call. We hated to seem selfish, but it was important!

Bud and I waited there a long time before the phone finally rang. Hurriedly I answered with the notes in my hand.

I could hardly believe what he told me! "The Channel 47 newsmen have just left Fresno for Squaw Leap to interview Scott's parents up there." Oh my, I should have stayed where I was, and the newsmen would have come to me. Who would ever have expected that?

"Now, what was it you wanted to say on T.V.?" It wasn't too late after all! So, in my best conversational tone, I read what was scrawled on the shopping list paper, and Chet said he'd put it on the air. That was easier than I had expected, and I laughed to think that no one would see how I looked after all.

I was already in town now, so I might as well go to the house. Bud and I got into the truck and headed that direction.

"How about a hamburger; can you use one?" Bud asked with a lilt in his voice.

"I'm really not hungry." It wasn't like me.

"Well, even if you're not, I'm starved to death! Here's a drive-in and I'm going to stop. Sure you can't eat anything? I think you should."

I wasn't in the mood to argue. "O.K. I'll take one."

Bud emerged a few minutes later with a Big Mac and a drink for each of us. "It's on me," so I thanked him.

The news team arrived at Squaw Leap early that afternoon. After taking pictures of the surroundings and the sheriff's search equipment, the reporter approached Joel for an interview.

The first question was a real winner: "How are you feeling today, Mr. Warkentin?"

How should he answer that, with the cameraman staring at him ready to video-tape whatever he said? Should he say how he really felt? He really didn't feel like answering a probing interviewer's question. Then he decided that he was on camera and he'd better say this right!

After briefly collecting his thoughts, Joel replied, "Of course we wish with all our hearts that Scott will be found. But the whole thing is in God's hands; my wife and I have turned it over to Him."

5

POSSES, ROCK CLIMBERS, AND A HELICOPTER

Joel spent the rest of Monday afternoon at the parking lot to greet and direct friends who were arriving to offer help. The word was getting around. Our son-in-law, Rick, was in the hills scouring the area along the river again in the afternoon. Although slimly built, he had a strong body, was a good hiker, and had an abundance of patience. We were pleased with the husband our Renetta had married.

About thirty-five mounted deputy sheriffs, some from Fresno County and others from Madera County, were out in two posses to check the locality. The riders traveled in pairs, each with a radio. The Madera County ground search team also joined in, because the land across the river was in that county. The river was the dividing line, so we had the two counties cooperating with us in the endeavor.

Professional rock climbers scaled the deep granite sides of the river, examining every crevase, cave, and bend for a clue.

The parking lot was now crowded with horse trucks, trailers, and sheriff department vehicles.

Two of our sons, Wayne and Ralph, were wandering around near the river calling, "Scott, Scott," everywhere they went. It was surprising to see what a wild place this turned out to be—so full of hidden gullies and ravines.

Suddenly Wayne stopped in his tracks.

"Ralph," he whispered, "did you hear that?"

"Yes," Ralph answered softly, in awe. "Someone said 'Hey!' and it's coming from down in the canyon. There, I just heard it again. Wayne, someone's down there!" He raised his voice. "It must be Scott! It sounds just like him. He sounds desperate!"

Although Wayne wasn't quite that sure, both boys were very excited as they scurried to try to follow the voice. The whole search might soon be over! Oh, what an ordeal it had been.

"Scott!" Ralph called again. "Scott. we've found you! Answer again so we can come to where you are!" And then he turned to his brother, "Wayne, I don't hear him anymore. I know he's around here somewhere. "Scott, answer me!" he yelled as loudly as he could.

There was nothing but silence. A bird twittered. They kept listening—nothing.

"We'll just have to go down there," Wayne admitted, heading in that direction.

The whole place was thick with brush, but it looked only like smooth grass until they tried to plow through it.

As the young men trudged along, suddenly right in front of them was a waterfall that went down about fifteen feet. They hadn't even noticed it until they almost fell in. There were smaller hidden falls and drop-offs everywhere.

Minutes turned into an hour or more as Scott's two brothers scoured every inch of the vicinity several times over. Scott surely must be there, but they just couldn't find him.

Finally both boys agreed they had to give up, thoroughly convinced that they had looked everywhere.

Just then Wayne spotted two fellow searchers nearby. As the men approached, he called them over. How interested they were to hear of the brothers' experiences!

"In these mountains," one of the strangers explained, "it's common to get a lot of real strange and unusual echoes. We're both very familiar with these parts, and we ought to know. That's probably what you heard."

As darkness fell Monday evening, the search effort was concluded for the day. Joel went to Renetta and Rick's place to spend the night and to be nearer the scene. Rick was an aluminum awning installer, and a very competent do-it-yourself man around the house. He was presently building a large garage

Lost, But Not Forever

and workshop for their home. Rick and Renetta were also foster parents for three teen-age girls. It's a thing they felt God wanted them to do. They lived in a spacious four-bedroom home situated in the foothills at the back of a five-acre undeveloped plot of hilly land. Big old oaks dotted the countryside—a beautiful and relaxing place for Joel to try to unwind.

But that night it rained all night long! Was Scott out in it? Alone in my bed at home, my thoughts were endless. What was he doing? How was he handling this? Oh, how I wanted to be there to help him! Surely he'd have enough sense to find shelter somewhere under a bush or boulder. But it was pouring so! Scott was wearing a good heavy coat, but that would get soaked through if he depended on it for rain protection, even for a short time; then he'd be drenched to the skin! Scott—as any boy—was never particular about keeping himself dry, yet he caught colds easily. "I mustn't worry!" Over and over I had to tell myself this. It doesn't do a bit of good. Worry is like a rocking chair—always agitated and moving, but never getting anywhere.

I thought of what I often said to others to encourage prayer as a substitute for worry. "The Bible says, 'Be careful for nothing,' which means not to be full of care about anything. And God goes on to say, 'but in everything by prayer and supplication with thanksgiving let your requests be made known unto God. And the peace of God, which passeth all understanding, shall keep your hearts and minds through Christ Jesus' (Philippians 4:6-7). God gives us an alternate to worry. In the most difficult situations we can pray about things instead of worrying over them. It is easier said than done, but prayer does accomplish for us what we ourselves cannot possibly hope to do. 'The effectual fervent prayer of a righteous man availeth much.'"

I had told all this to others so many times, and I believed it with all my heart. Now I was having to preach to myself, and I was having a difficult time doing it. My motherly instincts were hard to repress. With a great effort at this time, I tried to exercise my faith and surrender my son -wherever he was—into the arms of God's loving care. I was lying in a soft bed, warm

Mary Jane Warkentin

between clean sheets, but what about Scott? Usually I liked the sound of rain pattering on the roof. But not now! I should pray instead of worry. But I had prayed so much! It was time for God to start answering, and it seemed as if He wasn't responding to my many petitions. Nevertheless, regardless of what God was or was not doing, I told my Lord that I trusted Him. Since I could do nothing to supply the needs of my son, whatever they might be, I entrusted him—in the rain—into the care of my Father in heaven.

I recalled the time recently when Joel, Scott, and I hiked through the desert to an oasis. After a long, rugged climb, we had reached a beautiful spot where quiet pools of crystal-clear water blended with tall stately palm trees. How we relished that refreshing splash! Then I found that the ground was entirely covered with sharp, jagged stones—very difficult to navigate over such a rocky terrain. I needed something to hold onto! I came to a large, upright boulder and pressed my hands against it, discovering to my great satisfaction that walking was easy when leaning upon a big rock. It made a good illustration, so I persuaded my husband to take a picture of me to use in my Bible teaching. "If we lean on the Rock, Christ Jesus, we can go through any difficulty" I emphatically stated. Little did I realize then that less than two weeks later I would be leaning very heavily on that Solid Rock!

Tuesday dawned another rainy day. Early in the morning the authorities notified us that there was really nothing untrained helpers could do that day to assist in the search. Rock climbers were again going to comb the river gorge from the bridge all the way to Millerton Lake, which was about a five-mile stretch. Mounted posses would ride over the countryside. Sheriff's deputies would be attending base operations at the parking lot, with radio contact to the posses and climbers. It sounded well covered.

Lost, But Not Forever

If we lean on the rock Christ, Jesus, we can go through any difficulty.

Mary Jane Warkentin

So family members and friends went to their jobs or classes—except Joel. He preferred to stay in the Squaw Leap parking lot. Before leaving for the valley the previous day, a family friend had given Joel her Bible, saying, "Maybe this will give you some comfort." Sitting there in his Chevrolet station wagon—with the rain streaming down the windows—Joel felt sad, alone, and tearful. It had now been two days since he had seen Scott.

He picked up the Bible that lay on the seat of the car and turned to Psalm 37. The verses on submission to the Lord deeply impressed Joel during those rainy hours. It said, "Trust in the Lord...Delight thyself also in the Lord...Commit thy way unto the Lord...Rest in the Lord, and wait patiently for him: fret not thyself." No longer were they just words retained in his memory from years gone by. When he read "The steps of a good man are ordered by the Lord," he cried out, "Lord, God, Scott is as good a boy as they come. Surely if you guide anyone's steps, you will guide his!" Joel began to look into his own life. He felt that he was committed to God, but could it be that there was some area of his life that was not yielded? It was a time of real introspection. "Search me, O God, and know my heart: try me, and know my thoughts" (Psalm 139:23) cried Joel's anguished soul. "Remove O Lord, anything not pleasing to You."

Joel felt discouraged because the rain was washing away Scott's footprints. How could the searchers find him if his footprints were gone? Why was God letting this happen?

My husband remembered a prayer meeting some years before. The thought had been expressed that too often we have an escape hatch for our faith by saying, "If it is God's will." It was said that we should not let God off the hook that easily. We should say, "God, do it!" and then believe that He will perform the request. Was that what he should do? Was that right?

Joel decided to pray that way. "By the time it is dark, Lord, Scott is to be found, if he is alive. If he is no longer alive, then his body is to be found today."

Lost, But Not Forever

By afternoon the rain stopped. Ralph arrived from the valley, even though the authorities had discouraged volunteer help that day. He had tried to work. Usually he liked driving his little red pickup to car lots soliciting side-moulding or pin-striping jobs. Then he got a kick out of sprucing up the sharp new cars from the showroom floors! It was his first real taste of independence—making his own way in life, and he felt good about it.

But that day, after struggling with his job for a while, he concluded that he couldn't work with his little brother out there in the mountains. How could he eat good food when Scott hadn't eaten anything for two days? So Ralph laid down his tools and came to Squaw Leap to again join the search among the rocks and ravines in places where the professionals were not looking.

A large helicopter from an Air Force base arrived in the afternoon. It started combing the river area almost immediately. Before I knew it was coming, I had thought that a helicopter would be useful. It could fly very low with Ralph or me inside to call out over a microphone, "Scott, come out and answer! Come from where you are hiding, if you can. We are here to rescue you!" Maybe our familiar voices would make a difference. But before I was able to make this suggestion, the helicopter was flying without us.

Then Renetta came up with her cheerful little baby, Matthew. Joel's spirits were lifted to some extent. He and Renetta decided to take the mile walk down to the river, with Matthew in his mother's backpack. At the bridge they met a volunteer searcher and his dog. The man was a complete stranger who had heard on the news about the lost boy and wanted to help. Joel's feelings for his fellow man were heightened as he watched this compassionate helper and his faithful companion head up the ridge.

As they were returning to the parking lot, two teachers from Joel's school met them. Again he was greatly encouraged, realizing that these men were leaving their classroom duties to help him in this time of need.

However, when darkness fell, the rock climbers returned. No boy had been found.

The mounted horsemen returned without Scott.

The helicopter had seen nothing unusual.

All the searchers returned.

Deputy Sheriff Artie Cox announced that his superior in the Fresno County Sheriff's Office had decided that Scott must have fallen into the river and drowned, and that there was no further point in continuing the search. Joel felt that Artie really had wanted to find Scott, and had fully expected that he would be found. Now the deputy expressed his sympathy that it had turned out as it had, and hoped that Scott's body would be found for a proper burial.

Joel's mind raced. "That's not what I asked of God! I prayed earnestly, with a clean heart, that Scott would be found today—dead or alive—and he wasn't. Now what? Does God really care about our individual concerns?"

It was a terrible blow! He could have thrown all his beliefs into the wastebasket right then. "How can my faith still hold in a time like this?" he pondered.

Then amid the struggle, a familiar biblical passage emerged into Joel's thinking: "For my thoughts are not your thoughts, neither are your ways my ways, saith the Lord. For as the heavens are higher than the earth, so are my ways higher than your ways, and my thoughts than your thoughts" (Isaiah 55:8-9).

"I don't understand, God!" Joel silently confessed, "but I will continue to trust You; You know best." Out of it all came a new sense of surrender to God's will and way. Joel learned that he was to ask in faith, believing God would answer. But then he should leave it to God's perfect wisdom to decide what He will do. Joel agreed to accept whatever his Lord might choose for him.

6

SCOTT'S FIELD OF FLOWERS

Joel and Ralph again went to Renetta and Rick's to spend the night. In the evening, when supper was over, Joel and Rick (with baby Matthew) made themselves as comfortable as they could in the living room. Ralph and his sister stepped outside and sat on the front porch to talk about Scott. Renetta had been married and away from home for several years, and felt that she no longer knew her brother Scott very well. She wanted to know more about what he was like now that he was a teen-ager, what he thought, and how he spent his time. Ralph, on the other hand, had lived at home with Scott until recently, and those two were very close.

"One of Scott's favorite things is writing." Ralph began. "He scribbles off ficticious stories, histories, and even constitutions. Scott can do this by the hour on half-used paper that Dad brings home from school. He is also fascinated with maps. He likes to study them, or draw ones of his own. He enjoys his world globe and sometimes plays games with it. Scott will give it a whirl, and then ask anyone who is nearby to guess the country on which his finger will land when the globe stops. He has us memorizing the names of all those African nations!"

"Does he go in for sports?"

"Oh yes," said Ralph, "he likes baseball, also making up ball games with his own rules, which he plays by himself or with me in the back yard. We play catch, or soccer, and have foot or bike races. Dad always says that he's growing kids instead of grass! Even Mom likes to play tennis and ping-pong with Scott."

Ralph glanced out over the surrounding hills in the distance as the fading gleams of sunlight gave them a mysterious hue.

Renetta's brother went on: "In the evenings we play table games or ball games on paper with baseball cards. At times he tries to teach us what he's learning in school—Spanish,

Mary Jane Warkentin

geography, or grammar. Scott insists on giving us oral tests, or he likes us to ask him questions about Tom Sawyer or some other book he might be reading. And he never tires of the Guiness Book of World Records.

"When his friend from across the street comes over or he goes there, they have a great time acting out a dramatic production of an outer space episode, or some other exciting tale which they make up on the spot.

"He always had a big imagination. There's no one else like him.

"Scott doesn't let us in on his personal thoughts too much," Ralph admitted. "But he did say one thing that I thought was pretty great. He said that he was settled in his mind as to how he would live. He was sure that a Christian life was the best, and that was the way he intended to go. He was not even going to try anything else.

"Material things mean so little to Scott. He seldom spends any of his money. Why, he was more excited over the devotional times we had by candlelight with the family each evening at Christmas-time than he was over the exchange of presents. What a kid!

"Scott and I always have good times together. I'm his best friend, and I'm sure Mom is next best. He feels better with us than with anyone else. We do a lot of things together. I like thinking about it. If anyone happens to think that Scott would run away from home they're crazy, because that is his very favorite place to be."

Renetta was satisfied. She too liked having that kind of a brother. But she wondered—was he still alive? It was terrible not to know! Could it be that he had passed from this life to the Great Beyond? If that was so, her little Matthew would never remember Uncle Scott. She shrank from such a thought. Scott and Matthew had a real liking for each other. At every family gathering Matthew seemed drawn to Uncle Scott more than to anyone else. Matthew would crawl over to him while Scott, in a sweet boyish voice, would say, "Hi, Matthew. Hello, Matthew,"

Lost, But Not Forever

Scott with baby Matthew

Mary Jane Warkentin

repeating it over and over. The little fellow always seemed to like this. Renetta expressed fearful regret that this relationship might not be able to continue.

About 10:30 P.M. Joel and Ralph headed for the spare bedroom. Joel took the bed, and Ralph bedded down in a sleeping bag on the floor. Despite his agony, Joel finally fell asleep—only to be awakened by someone entering the room. It was Rick. "Dad, the sheriff's department wants to talk with you on the telephone."

Joel sat up straight, and immediately brought himself to his senses. The sheriff's department! What do they have to say? Joel quickly spotted the phone in the dim light and strode over to it. Have they found Scott? Or perhaps his body. Thoughts raced wildly.

Renetta jumped out of bed and anxiously rushed to her father's side, with Ralph close behind.

"I want to apologize for calling so late," the man on the line began, "but I thought you would like to know." Joel listened intently while the others wondered what he was saying. "A man has just called," he continued to say slowly, "evidently after watching the eleven o'clock news, to report that <u>his</u> was the party with the boy on the rock. The lad was safely removed by his own group before the deputies arrived."

"Oh," said Joel before hanging up. "I appreciate so much your calling and giving us this information."

"What did he say?" Renetta couldn't wait to ask. Joel told them all that the boy on the rock had not been Scott. Well, at least part of the puzzle was solved— a very small part.

"Then he's out there!" Renetta squealed exuberantly. "He's got to be out there!" They all grabbed and hugged each other and jumped around. The next morning they'd get out and find him for sure! They had been so afraid that the boy on the rock was Scott, and that he had fallen off and drowned in the river. Now they were all psyched up to try again! It was the first and only concrete information anyone had heard. Even though it was late at night, Joel called on the phone to tell me the news.

Lost, But Not Forever

But, the next day I saw an article in the newspaper that read:

Youth Feared Drowned

The search continued today for 15-year-old Scott Warkentin of Fresno, who disappeared Sunday in the wilderness area of Squaw Leap.

Sheriff's search and rescue teams scoured an area near the San Joaquin River, where the boy is believed to have been last seen. At the day's end, authorities believed the boy fell in the river and was killed.

They're satisfied that he's nowhere but in the river. He is believed to have fallen in the river and is believed dead.

That's exactly what it said! It was shocking. My head began to reel. A jumble of anger and confusion filled my mind, and I was unwilling to accept what I had read. How can anyone come to such a rash conclusion so soon? There are all kinds of other things that could have happened. They've only been looking for two days! It left me deeply hurt and disappointed. "If Scott is injured and lying under a bush, he might starve to death while all the town assumes that he drowned in the river," I said to myself madly. "Scott isn't the daring type at all! He's a chicken! He would never get close enough to a raging current to fall in! Why, he knows danger when he sees it!"

The thought of anyone imagining such a thing was repulsive to me. Joel and I had always been extra cautious with our children around water. It just wasn't logical that Scott would fall into a river, not in my book anyway.

It bothered me as I thought that our son was such a shy person, because I wasn't quite sure what he would do, except that he wouldn't fall into a river. I wondered if this were why no one had found him. For instance, he just might sit in a cave watching the airplanes fly by, thinking that he was not important—surely no one would be trying to find him. And they'd miss him. Or, if he heard someone call his name, would he answer? It may seem strange, but he often didn't answer on the school-ground. He was so shy. Such thoughts plagued my mind. Everyone said that Scott was a very intelligent boy, yet he was withdrawn. Only at home with his family did Scott really feel comfortable. With us he was very happy, and almost too talkative! But I wasn't sure how he would react in a strange situation. Yet, on the other hand, he could surprise us!

Drowned in the river? No, he couldn't be. But it was in the paper that Scott had drowned. All the Fresno County searchers had given up! Were they right?

However, Matt Markle, search leader of Madera County across the river, reacted like I did after hearing that Scott was assumed dead. "We don't accept that as an absolute conclusion," he proclaimed. "We intend to continue!" Now he was the man in charge.

So, in spite of my terrible fears that everyone was going to desert us, an intensive search went on the the next day. Most were volunteers. About thirty from our church helped, taking off from work or school to join in the effort. The territory was mapped out, and teams were assigned to check every ravine, under every bush, and behind each rock. Joel's fellow teachers came again, Rick's relatives, family, friends, even strangers. The Madera County Sheriff's Department had men in the field. The helicopter was back in the air, thoroughly combing the entire region. Matt was manning the radio headquarters at the parking lot. A tall, confident man, Matt was well acquainted with the area and knew the ranchers living in the vicinity. He was courteous and kind, taking a personal interest in the case. His manner brought great assurance to our family in such a time of stress. "I'll be glad to set anything aside if you need me," he said, and we knew he meant it. Surely with all this activity, it would be just a matter of a short time and someone would have some good results.

I hadn't wanted to stay at home away from the action, but it was evident that someone was needed there. I had a sample of

Lost, But Not Forever

Scott's tennis shoes sent to the mountains for Rick and the searchers to see. They needed other things from the valley besides food and drink—bandaids, raincoats, better hiking shoes. The task wasn't all done in the hills; I had a vital part to play, too.

Joel started out that day in a team with Ralph and a few friends. Somehow he became separated from the others. He was alone. Impulsively he dropped to his knees and agonized, crying out to God and imploring Him: "Oh Lord, give me a boy or give me a corpse. Let's settle this once and for all!" Then, again he remembered that the Creator of the universe had this whole situation in His hand, and He must be trusted.

Soon Joel looked up and began walking again, covering many more miles, checking ravines. In one place he stepped on a large solid-looking boulder. The rock rolled, knocking him to the ground and inflicting a wound on his hand. It could have pinned his leg down! Had something like this happened to Scott? Was he pinned down in some ravine? He certainly could be.

My husband decided that, since he was alone, he'd better stick to the beaten path. It wouldn't help for him to become the object of a search party! So he headed back toward the bridge and parking lot through a natural garden of beautiful wild flowers. How pleasant this would be, he mused, if it were not for the circumstances.

About three-fourths of the way around the Loop Trail, Joel came upon such a gorgeous field of flowers that he was moved to stop and admire it. A strong feeling came over him that Scott must have left this earth for the "land that is fairer than day." So he paused for a time to dedicate in prayer this beautiful field to the memory of Scott. Tears flowed, but a sense of the closeness to the Heavenly Father gave Joel an inner peace.

A bit farther along the trail Joel met Rick and Renetta. His daughter said, "Dad, they are concerned about you. Everyone says what a fast hiker you are, but all the others were back and you weren't there." Tearfully he told Renetta about dedicating

Mary Jane Warkentin

the field of flowers to Scott. He asked them to pause at the flower field and say a prayer in Scott's memory before they returned. Her loving embrace was a real comfort to Joel.

"We'd like to use dogs tomorrow," Matt informed Joel when he got back, "but we can't get any dogs unless we have some evidence that Scott may be around somewhere. So far we don't have a single clue. Something tangible will have to show up today." Almost everyone had left by now.

Dogs! That was exactly what I was hoping for! Dogs can smell out a person wherever he is; I was sure of it. But where were we to get the clue? No clue today—no dogs tomorrow! And it was already late in the afternoon—hopeless.

Back at home, with a mother's concern, I prayed. "Dear Lord God, I know you have all the power in the world; You know everything, and You are all-loving. You can see the end from the beginning. Lord, we put this whole predicament into your hands. We want them to find a clue today. Please God! I know the day is about over now! We want Scott to be found. God, You know that dogs would help! Dogs would probably find him! But dear Lord, whatever You want. That will be the best. We want Your will more than anything else." And I meant that—from the bottom of my heart I meant it.

Joel and I had both been Christians since we were young. We had asked Jesus into our lives when we realized that we needed forgiveness, that we were unable to help ourselves. Both of us had always tried to live good moral lives, but the time came when we understood that no one is good enough for heaven on his own. That's why Jesus Christ paid the penalty of sin for us by dying on the cross. I had said to God, "I am trusting You to guide me through this life, and I am depending upon the finished work of Christ on the cross to cleanse me, and to make me acceptable for heaven someday." Though miles apart, and seperated by some years, Joel and I had each eagerly invited Jesus into the deepest recesses of our hearts and asked Him to be our Savior and Lord. This had started us on a new life! The

Lost, But Not Forever

Bible expresses it: "If any man be in Christ, he is a new creature: old things are passed away; behold, all things are become new" (2 Corinthians 5:17).

We had already enjoyed this Christian life for many years. Jesus had become "sweeter as the years go by," as the old song says. He had been with us, as our friend and guide, through thick and thin, through the many difficulties of raising five children. Although there may have been times when we doubted, we knew for sure now that He was there. "He careth for you" is in the Bible (1 Peter 5:7)! Through many years of experience we had learned that God's ways are always best, even at times when it does not appear that way. He knew what He was doing, and He could be trusted. He is God! Whenever this word "God" is used it is meant to include the Father, Jesus, and the Holy Spirit—one Almighty God. We both loved this God, and truly wanted whatever would bring glory to Him. There was no mistake about it—we could now honestly say, "Thy will be done."

Another day ended, and Joel decided to return home to me, having spent Monday and Tuesday night at Renetta's house. The red Chevrolet station wagon had been left unlocked at Squaw Leap day and night with a note on it for Scott, in case he arrived at the parking lot tired and cold. Joel now wondered, however, whether or not our Heavenly Father had Scott in His arms. If so, his dear fifteen-year-old would not need the shelter of a car to keep him warm and dry.

7

AT LAST A SIGN

During the day while an army of volunteers were serving us in the mountains, I had a decision to make at home. The next night I was expected to lead a once-a-month devotional at Evangel Home as I always did on my night. It seemed like such an intrusion into our one important task of finding Scott. Yet I couldn't completely neglect this responsibility. If I were to cancel, I would need to do it now. And yet, was there a possibility that I could go ahead as usual—stand up in front of people and talk—in my condition?

Evangel Home is a temporary home for women and children who need emergency shelter in a loving and caring Christian atmosphere. Outsiders come daily to direct the women in a time of devotions. The message presented to them is: "Christ alone is able to give new direction to your life, and is the only sure foundation on which to build; He can lift up the fallen and break the bonds of sin, discouragement, and despair." The old song is often sung at Evangel Home:

> Out of my shameful failure and loss,
> Jesus, I come, Jesus, I come;
> Into the glorious gain of Thy cross,
> Jesus, I come to Thee;
> Out of Earth's sorrows into Thy balm,
> Out of life's storms and into Thy calm,
> Out of distress to jubilant psalm,
> Jesus, I come to Thee.

I wanted to go! Yes, my son was lost in the mountains and I might break down crying in the middle of it all. But, although tears were always close to the surface these days, it was my turn to give a talk and I wanted to do it. Renetta had once

Lost, But Not Forever

commented to me that God just loves to use unlikely people! Surely that was true in my case. I am an emotional person, and have always cried easily. By nature I'm a listener and a follower. Yet God has promised, "I can do all things through Christ which strengtheneth me" (Philippians 4:13). He could use me!

As I was thinking about it, the phone rang, and surprisingly Marabelle, the superintendent of Evangel Home, was on the line. "Mary Jane. I want you to know that I will be glad to take your place and fill in for you tomorrow night," she offered.

"Oh, thank you. That makes me feel better," I answered. "I may need to call on you. But if God gives me the composure to do it, I would like very much to tell the ladies what I am going through, and how wonderful the Lord has been to me in the midst of it all. I feel that I have a vital message to bring, and I want to try to do it. I'd like it if you'd be in the wings ready to take over, if I need you. Sometimes I feel very weepy, and other times I'm stronger. I'll have to wait until the last minute to know. If God wants me to come, won't He make me able to do it?"

Marabelle assured me that He would. "Maybe we need a few more tears around here anyway," she added, although I was not quite ready to agree right then.

I thought when she hung up, "I could have easily gotten out of doing that. But maybe my story can help someone, and I might miss that opportunity if I don't go."

The front door flew open—my family was home from the mountains! Joel, Wayne, and Ralph, all well over six feet, walked into the room, obviously dead tired. But they sure looked good to me! Donald, our other son, was still in school taking a final exam. I was especially happy to see my husband after two and a half days of absence! We all had a big hug for each other.

"Everybody was out searching for Scott today," Joel told me. "There must have been close to a hundred people swarming the place. I couldn't believe some of them who came to hunt for our son! One big executive took off work to stomp around up there.

Mary Jane Warkentin

A few girls were trudging through the rough terrain. Rick said that he was so tired that he could hardly stand up at the end of the day. By the way, Scott's tennis shoe pattern did not match any footprints Rick or anyone had seen.

"A couple of guys got lost. They weren't supposed to separate, but it's practically impossible in some places, as you can't see each other even a few feet apart."

"Yeah, I know!" added Wayne. "I was in a group who were walking Indian style with a deputy in front. No one else saw a tent that we walked past. I was the last one in the line, and when I pointed it out to the rest of them, they were amazed that anything that big could be so well hidden in the underbrush. That's the kind of a place it is up there."

"Once we heard a gun shot," Joel continued. "We thought it meant they had found something, and we should all go back. But then I remembered that the rule is to fire twice. We didn't hear a second shot, so we decided that it wasn't anything after all."

Ralph wanted to say something. He had been trying to hold back his enthusiasm until his family finished talking, but obviously he had something very important to tell.

"But guess what someone did find!" he finally blurted out. "Look at this!" He produced a paper plate with some Xs and lines penciled on the back. "This is a pattern drawn from some markings the searchers found on the ground. They had no paper up there, so they copied it down on the back of this paper plate. The deputies think Scott may have done it!"

A soft squeal burst forth from my lips, as I took the plate in my hands and looked closer to study the markings.

They didn't make any sense.

Lost, But Not Forever

```
X            X            X ———— X  〰〰
X            X            X ———— X
X ———— X ———— X ———— X
```

I looked at Ralph questioningly.

"They're not sure what it's supposed to mean," he said, "but it was found on the other side of a fenced area. All the Xs are sticks put into the ground in an upright position, and the lines were scratched into the dirt with rocks. This on top is a scuff mark, like someone was trying to erase something, or maybe identify a certain place—I don't know what! Anyway, they say it's a clue, and if they believe Scott may have done it, they will call in the dogs."

I looked hard at the diagram, turning it this way and that, but it was still confusing...until a thought hit me: "Could it be?" I said aloud, "maybe..no..yes, it could—it could be the Big Dipper." I studied it again. "The scuffed up place? That shows where you are to look in the direction of the North Star. What do you think?"

Everyone tried to look at it at once.

"You may be right," Joel considered. "Scott could have stayed at that place the first night. When it got dark, he looked up into the sky at the Big Dipper, then tried to make the pattern with sticks in the ground so he would know for sure the next day which way was north. Home would be south-west from there. Scott always drew things very roughly; yes, it could be."

I added, "That fits perfectly with what we heard from the ranger when we were camping at Joshua Tree National Monument." Just the week before, Joel, Scott and I had been attending a campfire program on astronomy. Besides viewing the stars and their moons or rings through a telescope, diagrams were flashed on a screen in lights, showing various constellations. A highlight was how to find directions from the

North Star and the Big Dipper, and Scott obviously had enjoyed it. It was fresh in his mind.

At home a few days after that, a neighbor had seen Scott out in the front yard after dark staring at the sky.

"What's wrong with Scott?" the kid asked.

"Oh, he's just checking out the Big Dipper," Donald had told him.

Scott would certainly be looking at the bright stars if he were alone at Squaw Leap, and perhaps planning his strategy for the next day. Wayne was of the opinion that the diagram did not look the least bit like the Big Dipper; nevertheless, hope was again revived that Scott might be alive.

"Let's tell Matt about this!" I exclaimed enthusiastically. "If Scott didn't do it, it might be what's needed for the dogs to come, and then they will find him." It was the answer to my prayer that I prayed so late in the afternoon. It was still the same day! Besides, we weren't sure—it could indeed have been Scott's work!"

Joel made the call.

"Dogs will be flown in first thing in the morning," Matt announced.

"Whoop-ti-doo!!" I shouted loudly, using an expression that I reserved only for the most exciting occasions. When had I heard such good news?

Because dogs would be there, the authorities did not want anyone else in the vicinity the next day. The dogs could sniff out a human presence within a three-hundred-foot radius. It was important that they not be distracted with other scents. The whole place would be patrolled so no one could enter.

"Oh my," I sighed. "All day I've been encouraging people to go up and help tomorrow! When calls come in and someone wants to help in some way, I've been telling them to meet you at 9:00 A M. in the parking lot. I thought that was our plan."

"It was. And you did good work," Joel smiled at me sweetly. "But now we'll have to call them all back because the circumstances have changed. And, just in case the dogs don't

Lost, But Not Forever

find Scott in two days, we'll need all the workers we can get on Saturday."

I couldn't imagine anything like that; of course they'll find him—if he's there.

The evening was spent on the telephone, but this time Joel did most of the talking.

The next day, soon after dawn, the phone rang. Joel was already up, so he answered it. He listened a few seconds and then called very excitedly, "Mary Jane!" He was almost in tears with emotions. I jumped out of bed and ran to his side. He was still on the phone. "The dogs have found Scott! They have found Scott!" he yelled to me. I could hardly believe it. I glanced at the wall clock; yes, it was time that the dogs would be out there running. And they found my sweet boy! I was stunned.

"What...?" Joel said into the phone. There was a prolonged pause and his face fell, "Oh, all right. Thank you for calling."

It was a mistake. The newscast had said the dogs were there looking, not that they had found anything.

Joel stayed home all that day. He was emotionally exhausted.

8

THE BIBLE SAYS SO

I stumbled back into bed after that early Thursday morning phone episode. Now it was very hard to accept the idea that Scott was still out there, and that things were no different from the way they were. My dear boy had not been found by the dogs! We would have to start all over again...I couldn't face it...or should we quit? Yet what if he <u>were</u> somewhere waiting for someone to find him?

I fell into a deep sleep. It was a long time before I saw the light of day again and tried to live some more with that same old empty feeling. I just lay there, slowly trying to make the transition to reality. Then I did arouse myself enough to quote my "morning poem" quietly. It was something I had composed in my youthful days—just for me. Maybe this would help set the mood for a better day.

> Oh, what a beautiful morning,
> After a night of sweet rest,
> For loving, for lifting—adorning
> For living with life at its best!
> Oh, let us not run in our own willful way—
> In search for a pleasure or two;
> If we walk by His side, He will surely provide
> And bring happiness all the day through!

It was a far cry from how I felt now, but it did get me out of bed.

While the trained police dogs that had been flown in were still trying to sniff out Scott's presence in a secluded spot, I knew that I must try to put my mind on the lesson and devotional time that I had said I would lead at Evangel Home that evening. I felt like calling Merabelle and saying that I wouldn't do it, but

Lost, But Not Forever

instead I sat down by the window with my Bible, a paper, and a pencil. I really did want to share what was happening in my own life. It wouldn't be the usual Bible study this time. But it shouldn't be just a story either. I would intersperse the story with Bible verses. As a strong believer in the power of God's written word, I knew the Holy Spirit would want to use the Bible in conveying this message to the ladies. How was I able to think of others when I was so down? Really, it did me good to try. I always loved to teach the Bible to a group. What a privilege to have listeners who would sit quietly and let me open up the marvelous truths of the Scriptures that thrilled me so. But why did it have to be on an awful day like this?

I began with a prayer for guidance. "Lord, open my eyes that I may behold wondrous things out of Thy law." Never did I begin preparations without acknowledging my utter dependence upon the Holy Spirit. If He does not take over with His power and presence, my efforts will fall flat, no matter how hard I try.

Soon thoughts began to come. Of course I would include "In all thy ways acknowledge him, and he shall direct thy paths" (Proverbs 3:6). I began looking further in the book of Psalms, where many favorite verses were already underlined. Old verses were popping out with new meaning!

"The Lord also will be a refuge for the oppressed, a refuge in times of trouble. And they that know thy name will put their trust in thee: for thou, Lord, hast not forsaken them that seek thee" (Psalm 9:9,10). So God had not forsaken Scott.

"Thou wilt show me the path of life" (Psalm 16:11). God could show Scott where the right path was.

"For thou art my rock and my fortress; therefore for thy name's sake lead me, and guide me" (Psalm 31:3).

"Thou art my hiding place; thou shalt preserve me from trouble; thou shalt compass me about with songs of deliverance" (Psalm 32:7). I really began to get excited reading these verses!

And how appropriate the next one was. "The young lions do lack, and suffer hunger; but they that seek the Lord shall not

Mary Jane Warkentin

want any good thing" (Psalm 34:10). A verse like that made me feel better.

Even "Give us this day our daily bread" (Matthew 6:11) took on new meaning. Usually I was in church on Sunday mornings when we quoted this part of the Lord's Prayer. My thoughts would go to the roast beef dinner baking in our oven at home as we said this verse. But now it was real! Scott needed daily bread! Water was no problem; it was everywhere up there. Little streams ran into bigger ones, with waterfalls and rivulets all over. But what about food? What was he eating? If only I knew whether or not he'd eaten anything! He was too thin already. Once at a baseball game when Scott had stood up to bat, I overheard someone say, "That's the skinniest kid I ever saw!" He had no extra fat; he wouldn't last long unless he were eating something.

As I reflected on it, God gave me real comfort in a strange way from the memory of an experience He had brought into our lives. While camping recently, we had gone on a little hike—a self-guided tour. Placards were placed at points along the way describing a bush, tree, or plant. The emphasis had been on how the Indians had lived and survived in this parched desert some years ago. They had used some of the leaves for tea. They ate flowers, stems, roots, and seeds. Some plants served as medicines, and there were other uses as well. Scott had been quite interested in this, and surely he had been impressed with the fact that a person can eat and be healthy on wild plants. "God prepared him for this," I mused.

Also, I thought of another time on the same trip when children—even little ones—were taking chances climbing high among the rocks. Seizing the opportunity to warn Scott, I had said, "Never take one chance, because it only takes one slip of the foot, and you're a goner from this world. Always test your footing first, and don't do anything that is the least bit dangerous." Scott listened; he was a sensible lad. I was so glad now that I had given him this warning.

Lost, But Not Forever

Yet that was not all. One time he came back to the campground and said he had been lost. He had wandered around, and finally spotted our van. "Be careful of things like that, Scott. Keep track of where you are in relation to our campground. Next time you may not be so lucky as to find your way back." He was already a young man, but I wanted him safe. Now as I thought on these things, it was a real comfort to know that I had given these admonitions to Scott so recently, even if it did seem somewhat over-protective. I had never put it to him that way before. It was good for my own consolation now, if for nothing else.

But I must get back to my studies I suddenly realized. My, how my mind had wandered! Quickly shifting mental gears, I flipped over to Psalm 34:19: "Many are the afflictions of the righteous: but the Lord delivereth him out of them all." If God wants Scott delivered, He will do it. The verse doesn't say we will always be spared from affliction, however.

Although I really didn't care at this time what happened to me —only that Scott be all right—still I ran across a verse that was just for me, "Why art thou cast down, O my soul? and why art thou disquieted within me? Hope thou in God: for I shall yet praise him for the help of his countenance" (Psalm 43:5). The other verses said that He would take care of Scott, but He also could quiet my anxious heart.

I couldn't believe how the book of Psalms could speak so clearly to my own situation! I had been led to such very comforting verses in the Bible. It seems that the greater your need is, the more the Bible speaks to you.

Yet there was still more: "God is our refuge and strength, a very present help in trouble" (Psalm 46:1). And "Be still and know that I am God" (Psalm 46:10). I needed that one!

There was a power in these verses that strangely filled me with peace, rest of heart, and yes, even a bit of joy! Bible verses are an important way that God speaks to us. How essential it is for Christians to hide these words in their hearts. I was so very glad that I knew the Bible well before all this happened, so the right parts could pop into my mind when I needed them. I was being royally fed by God's own hand, and at the same time was preparing to meet with the Evangel Home ladies that night. If only I didn't start crying thinking about it!

I went on. "Wow," I said half outloud when reading, "For this God is our God for ever and ever: he will be our guide even unto death" (Psalm 48:14).

That was enough. I put a check beside each one. Now I was ready—come what may—in case God decided He wanted to use me. I sat there longer, reflecting further on the whole predicament. "Why did God let Scott get lost?" I asked myself. "Surely He could bring much good out of such a situation. But what a thing for us all to have to endure!" I thought of people who had been sawed in two, or thrown to lions, or burned at the stake. All that was terrible. But it was over so soon! Death alone seemed mild beside the possible agony Scott could be going through, and the mental torture it brought to us not knowing.

The night before, I had dreamed that Scott had been found, but had a very high fever. I was sponging him down with a wet cloth, and he was feeling much better. Did he need that right now? Did he hurt? He must be so afraid and lonesome, wherever he was.

Our daughter, Renetta, had made the remark the day before that when Scott returned, he would really be a man. Wouldn't he, though! Maybe that's why God allowed this. Won't he have friends now, if he ever gets back!

All the boys will want to know, "Did you see any bears or wolves?"

"Where did you sleep—in a cave?"

"What did you eat?"

"Did you think you would ever get back?"

Then they'd all notice him, and it would build his self-confidence! This would bring him out for sure. That's it! I almost decided that was why God was letting Scott go through such an experience! Well, maybe not, I reconsidered. It could be that he will never be back to see how friendly people can be to him. Immediately I put such an idea out of my mind, and thought instead about how great it was that everyone rallied so for Scott in the effort to find him. Sometimes I had felt that no one even noticed him, but now look at the commotion that has been going on!

Also, he must certainly be learning to trust in God for himself. My, how he must be praying these days! He will be a spiritual giant when he returns! Perhaps God wants to use him in some mighty way someday and this is part of the preparation. Everyone the Lord uses has to go through something hard, I've often noticed.

"Thy will be done, oh God. And please use me tonight at Evangel Home, and prepare the hearts of the girls there. Send Your Spirit into that place, and speak to each one. Help me to carry on. But prepare Merabelle's heart if You want her to do it instead. In Jesus' name, I pray. Amen."

Although my lesson was ready, that afternoon my emotions hit bottom. It was so confusing, so hurtful, so bewildering to have my son somewhere and not know where—not to understand what was going on and why.

Joel had gone to buy a few things: a compass, another map, and a poncho. Ralph was at work and the other brothers were in school. By all appearances it was a normal day. I was alone at home, but very tired. The phone rang and rang. My vitality seemed to have ebbed away, and I was left drained and empty. Tears began to well up, and I let them come. I cried aloud—stopping just long enough to talk to the people who called on the phone. Turning tears on and off was getting to be too much.

Finally, exhausted, I walked out of the house, got foam pads from the garage, put them into the back of the van which was parked in the driveway, took my fluffiest pillow and a full box of kleenex, and locked myself inside. I felt dull, droopy, and spiritless. Let it ring—I wasn't there! Sinking into the foam pads like a floppy doll, I lay there languidly, with a gentle breeze

Mary Jane Warkentin

from the partly-opened window touching my hot, wet cheeks. Sobbing intermittently, I talked aloud with God...and with myself.

The first chapter of James came to my mind: "Let him ask in faith, nothing wavering. For he that wavereth is like a wave of the sea driven with the wind and tossed. For let not that man think that he shall receive any thing of the Lord" (James 1:6-7). Did I doubt all those verses I'd read in the Psalms that morning? They said that God delivers! I began to go through an experience similar to the one Joel had gone through earlier. I wrestled with my thoughts, trying to decide if I should demand an answer from God, or accept whatever comes. I was willing to pray either way, but was so confused. It may be that I should not say "if it is God's will" when I pray.

"Does God, or does He not want to save Scott from disaster?" I wondered. "Scott is God's child, and God loves him. God will care for him. Then it is His will, and I should pray without doubting! God, I believe it is Your will to rescue Scott. Do it! I believe You will do it! Oh, thank You. But if I am wrong in determining Your will, I accept whatever You have for me. I love You more, God, than I love anyone in the world. When all else is gone, You will still be there. You have said, 'I will never leave you nor forsake you.' That includes me, and it includes Scott." I was satisfied that the Lord had led me to pray in the right way.

For two hours I rested and prayed and wept and thought. Gradually I could feel a bit of strength re-entering my agonized body.

Slowly the sobs began to subside.

9

YOU COULD FEEL THE POWER OF THE SPIRIT

It would soon be time to leave for Evangel Home. As I thought about it, I was amazed that such a lovely home could be provided free of charge to anyone who needed it, solely from gifts of money by ordinary people who cared about others!

I had cried most of the afternoon and had been totally exhausted, but now you couldn't hold me back with a team of horses!

Merabelle called once more to offer her services as a substitute. "Thank you, but I'm planning to come," I declared. "I have a message, and I must give it."

Arriving at Evangel Home, I admired the attractive, modern, home-like building. Inside I found Merabelle and ten other ladies, along with a few children, were already seated about the parlor ready to hear my story. They had been told of the tragic situation, and were probably wondering what this mother would possibly think of to say about God on a night like this.

It seemed as if I were walking on holy ground. Would I be able to make them understand? As I stood and began to tell the experience of Scott's disappearance four days ago, I could feel the presence of the Holy Spirit in that room—more strongly than I had ever experienced it there before. God's power was behind the words as they flowed forth.

Relating the story from the beginning, I gave God the glory for His guiding hand in all events. I shared with them the verses that had blessed me so much that morning.

Going on, I told of my confusion in understanding what was happening, but that I knew I must yield everything into God's all-knowing, all-loving hands. I expressed my willingness to accept whatever the Lord had for our son, be it life or death, as hard as that was to do.

The room was very quiet, and the ladies were listening intently. I knew they were receiving the message more clearly than they would a theological Bible study. Why does it take something like this to touch people's hearts? Isn't the Word of God alone enough? But somehow these women were able to identify with a story of difficulty and stress, and the verses from the book of Psalms spoke to them.

Then I told the group about God's call for all of us to make a beginning with Him—to accept Jesus, His forgiveness, and His gift of salvation, whether we understand it all or not.

I led them in a prayer like this:

> Lord Jesus, I know I am a sinner. I have not done all that you have wanted me to do, and I confess this to You. I have failed in trying to run my own life. Come in and take over! Forgive me all my sins and shortcomings. I know You died on the cross so I could go free. Save me now! Make me over new the way You want me to be. I want You to be my Savior, and I thank You for it. Amen.

Throughout the meeting, I especially noticed one rather short, attractive young lady with tears gently flowing down her cheeks. "All this is too sad for them," I thought. "These girls have enough pain in their own lives. But, maybe the Holy Spirit is dealing with this young lady."

Driving home, I was thankful that the Lord had enabled me to share my story without breaking down. It really surprised me that I was able to compose myself, and I wondered at this evidence of God's power.

But now it was over, and I was anxious to return home and find out the latest report of the day's activities at Squaw Leap. I couldn't wait to hear if the dogs had accomplished anything! Could it be that God was reserving a time of rejoicing for me until after I had made that appeal at Evangel Home?

Lost, But Not Forever

Upon arriving at our house, I learned that neither of the police dogs had found anything. Two young women had run behind the dogs, holding onto their leashes. They thoroughly covered the territory within the Loop Trail and up the ridge in the area where the diagram had been found. But the dogs had picked up no scent. However, they would be called in Friday to run in a different direction.

I was now quite certain that Scott was not on any of the land where the animals had sniffed. He must have wandered further—unless he drowned in the river. If the latter were the case, his body would surface in a week or so, we were told. But we could not assume that he was dead; more remote spots would have to be investigated.

It was now Friday morning, and the phone was ringing. I hurried to answer it.

"This is the housemother at Evangel Home. I want to tell you some good news that I know will make you feel better."

"What is that?" I was ready for some good news.

"One of the girls who was at your devotional last night told me that she accepted the Lord."

"Oh really!" It did make me happy to know that God had actually used my struggling effort.

"Her name is Marcy," the housemother went on. She was sitting in the big armchair about in the middle. She's rather small, with short ash-blond hair—about thirty."

Yes, I knew immediately which one she meant. So the tears were ones of conviction!

"She said that as you were praying, she just let God into her life and His love flowed into her."

"Oh, that's great!" I answered with real enthusiasm. "Now I have a spiritual baby to nurture."

The following morning I hurried over to be with Marcy. I found that the strained face I had seen the night before was gone. A peace had settled in.

Mary Jane Warkentin

"How long have you been living here at the home?" I wanted to know.

"It's been two weeks," she answered softly, then she looked up at me with hazel-green eyes, and she knew I wanted to hear more. "Life was so unsettled," she went on to say. "It finally got so bad that I had nowhere to live, and I was very discouraged. Someone suggested I go to this home. I knew it was run by Christian people, and that they might ask me to receive Jesus Christ as my Savior, but I decided it would be all right. I wasn't stupid about God's plan of salvation; I'd just never done anything about it."

"Then if you were so open to becoming a Christian," I interrupted, "I should think you would have received Jesus into your life soon after you arrived here."

"I thought I would, too," Marcy explained, "but something terrible happened that kept me from it."

"What was that?"

Marcy's radiant face took on a sadder look. "It was an awful tragedy," she said. "You saw my ten-year-daughter last night. Well, a very close girl friend of hers, just a child, and such a pretty one..." It was hard for Marcy to go on.

"What happened to her?" I tried to help.

My new friend looked down as she said, "She died."

There was an awkward pause, but Marcy soon continued. "It made me so confused and angry. How could God allow the death of someone so young...if there were a god? It seemed like a cruel and heartless thing—so unexpected. It wasn't right for her to be an innocent victim in a drug-related car accident. My daughter kept asking me why it happened."

"And what did you tell her?"

"I didn't know what to say. I was mixed up myself, and there seemed to be no way to reconcile it all. Surely if there were a god, He was not a good god. So I refused the gospel of Jesus Christ."

"My!" I exclaimed, wondering how else to respond to what I was hearing. "But you did become a Christian last night?"

64

Lost, But Not Forever

"Yes, I did," she assured me with a smile that I was learning to love. Her whole being vibrated again with an effervescence that convinced me she had experienced a genuine conversion. "You were facing death, too, or at least possible death—not of a friend, but of your own offspring. Yet you didn't blame God or reject Him. Instead, He was helping you!"

I nodded in agreement.

"You said that you loved God more than you loved anyone, even your youngest son. I sensed your confidence that whatever God did was right, yet I knew it was only by the power of God that you could say, 'Thy will be done.' I realized that God has a purpose in all that He does. Perhaps He wanted to spare that little girl the heartaches of life in the drug-oriented environment of which her parents were a part. Suddenly I realized for sure that God must be real!"

Marcy had been touched by the fact that, in the midst of a personal tragedy, I was able to care about someone else, and she was sure that it was God Who gave me the ability to do this. I was no one special—just an ordinary lady—but I had been interested in Marcy. If I loved her, God loved her more. She was convinced right then that Jesus the Son of the living God, wanted to come into her life and give her a new beginning!

I had quoted the Bible verse that says, "For all have sinned, and come short of the glory of God" (Romans 3:23). She thought of her life. She had sinned: she was sure of that.

Then she heard, "For the wages of sin is death: but the gift of God is eternal life through Jesus Christ our Lord" (Romans 6:23). She really wanted that gift!

Finally, an old familiar verse sank deep into her heart: "For God so loved the world, that he gave his only begotten Son, that whosoever believeth in him should not perish, but have everlasting life" (John 3:16).

Mary's spiritual eyes were opened! Yes, this mother could trust such a God—and she did.

10

A DOG NAMED GRACE

The following day the police dogs were again unsuccessful, although for a time it appeared that they had found something. They headed for a spot where vultures had been seen flying to the ground, but they could find nothing there.

Rick and his cousin rode horses the same day in an adjoining locale, with no results.

Each new day began with high expectation; but when the day was gone, everyone felt uneasy that Scott was out there and had not been found. The day's hopes were crushed at darkness; perhaps tomorrow would be better. So everyone was quite ready for a big, all-out manhunt by volunteers on Saturday.

Friday night a long-distant call came from a stranger in a neighboring town. "I have a good bloodhound that I will let you use in the search for your boy," he informed us. "She can follow a trail, and she will find your son for you." It sounded good. Of course, dogs had been hunting for two days. but this dog functioned on a different principle. After being given a whiff of a sock or other clothing belonging to the victim, she would search for that odor and follow it.

However, the owner, Mr. Anderson, was seventy years old and did not have the endurance to run after the dog for long periods. He said he would be most happy to lend his dog, Grace, if there were someone who could keep up with her.

"I'll do it!" our son Donald offered immediately. He was a husky young college student—very athletic. Donald welcomed the assistance of a bloodhound. He called some friends, one of whom had been a track champion in high school. Wayne decided to go with them, too; his long legs and six-foot-four height would stand him in good stead. He also was a lover of the great outdoors.

Lost, But Not Forever

"I'll have Grace in the Squaw Leap parking lot at nine in the morning," the man said. It was settled.

I hurried to Scott's chest of drawers to find a dirty sock for the dog to smell, then to the clothes hamper. Alas, they had all been washed! His underwear? It had also gone through the laundry! It seemed a lost cause...until at last I thought of his pajama drawer. Scott always wore a pair of big red camping booties on his feet at night for warmth. They hadn't been washed since he disappeared, and probably for a good while before. The perfect thing! Breathing a sigh of relief, I carefully dropped one into a plastic bag and sealed it for the morning.

Joel and four others also started out the next morning in a brand new four-wheel-drive Trailbuster offered by a fellow employee. As they rode over some of the smaller roads, they decided to visit a few nearby ranch houses.

They found an eighty-four-year-old native of the area—a cattleman with a big Irish smile. He came out from his house when the men drove into his yard. Joel stated their business and he immediately was anxious to help. He knew about the boy being lost and told them that the posse had gone past his place. He suggested other spots where they might look. Ralph—also in a four-wheel-drive-vehicle provided by a fellow worker—had stopped at his house that day, and had been impressed by this man's big-heartedness.

His friends drove Joel to another ranch adjoining the Squaw Leap territory on the Madera side of the river. A cousin of Deputy Sheriff Mart Markle gave them immediate permission to go anywhere on his land to look for Scott! He said the helicopers had flown all over his place already, and the mounted posse had crossed his property. "The members of the posse know where all the old buildings are around here," he said, "and they have checked every one." That was good to know.

By being able to go on his land, Joel's group could pass to other regions, including a radio facility. The men scoured Kennedy Table and the terrain below. After walking to the north end of Kennedy Table, they could see all over the countryside.

Mary Jane Warkentin

Through field glasses they saw many others wandering about, probing through the underbrush.

This was an all-out effort—each one determined that he would be the one to find Scott, if indeed he were to be found.

They then came across a settlement along Finegold creek—a motley group of buildings in various stages of completion and composed of a variety of materials. Most of the walls were made of plywood, but old boards or thin stapled plastic also had been used. The buildings looked like a combination of old houses stuck together. Several small children paddled a raft on a big pond. A few cows and chickens wandered about.

Joel and the others began calling—no response. Finally two young men appeared, not violent-looking but definely drop-outs from traditional society. Ralph had been there also, but his younger brother had not.

Meanwhile at home, I was anxiously awaiting the arrival of my two sons, Donald and Wayne, after their day in the mountains with Grace, the big red bloodhound. Donald had not been engaged in the search before, because all this had caught him smack in the middle of college final exams.

While I was waiting, the phone rang. Joel's sister on the other end of the line asked in her usual quiet way, "Did you hear they are calling off the search?"

"Who is calling off the search?" I shouted—shocked and horrified!

"The Madera County Sheriff's Department. If Scott isn't found by six o'clock tonight, they're not going to look any longer."

I wouldn't believe it. "Where did you hear that?"

"It was announced on the radio just now," she answered. Station KBIF has reports on Scott every hour, you know; I always listen."

We were always so busy in the process of trying to find our boy that we seldom heard the newscasts. This was the moment I dreaded! So long as someone was looking and we still had

Lost, But Not Forever

leads, I was encouraged; but whatever would I do if everyone quit? What would I do? It scared me to death.

"Well, thank you for letting us know." That was all I could say. If the sheriffs give up, everyone else will, too! "How can I stand it?" I thought. I felt so alone.

Just then Donald and Wayne walked into the house. I grasped at a straw and asked them if the dog found Scott. I could tell by the look on their faces that she had not.

"Didn't she even find a trail to follow?" I had to get some positive answer out of them.

"Sure she did," Donald replied with a half-smile. "That dog found lots of trails."

"Really? Tell me about it."

Donald sat down in the reclining chair and pushed it way back. He knew I'd expect every detail, so Wayne and I settled ourselves on the couch while Donald related the experiences of the day with Grace.

"We began by making the dog smell Scott's old bootie for a long time," he said. "She didn't like to do it, and kept pulling her head away. But we insisted, and I'm sure she got a good whiff of it before we left.

"Then we started down the path from the parking lot. The owner was holding tightly onto the leash, and the dog was straining hard, anxious to go. Mr. Anderson said that Grace was following Scott's trail. Hikers had been walking there, and we thought she was onto those people's trails.

"After some distance, there was a little meadow. The dog slowed down, left the path, and sauntered into the field. 'She's just going around in circles,' we said.

"But Mr. Anderson was very positive. 'Scott must have walked around in that meadow for a while,' he explained.

"She took to the trail again, and it wasn't long before we came to that raging San Joaquin River. About halfway across the bridge, the old man asked me if I would like to take the lease. So I tried to hold the dog back while she bolted across the bridge. This was the last place that Dad had seen Scott the day

Mary Jane Warkentin

he left us. It's where Dad was sitting, and he told you, Mom, that Scott had gone ahead on the trail while he was taking pictures of the river and we haven't seen him since. The track runner and Wayne with his long legs, were close behind. She ran along the trail that goes up the ridge, the exact place where Dad last saw Scott six days ago. Then the dog left the path. We were all following in giant strides wherever Grace went.

"Darting underneath a little tree where a bunch of grass was matted down, she sniffed there a long time. 'That must be where Scott slept for the night,' panted Mr. Anderson. He was just now beginning to catch up with us. Actually, he did very well running for a man of his age!"

Sitting on the edge of my seat in our family room, I interrupted Donald to ask, "Or could that be where searchers might have sat?"

"That's possible," he answered, "but Mr. Anderson was very sure that Scott had been there, because his dog really did get excited under that trees! Well, then the bloodhound finally rambled on, following a trail of matted grass. There were very narrow spots where we could barely squeeze through the bushes. Tall grass was all around. We had to push branches back all over the place and fight our way through. What wild country!"

"All those branches hit you in the face?" I asked with concern.

"No, I brushed them aside before I got to them." He made it all sound so easy. "The dog kept running—down the cliffs, lunging through streams, crashing through bushes. She found more and more of those spots where it looked as though somebody had been sleeping."

"Was Mr. Anderson able to keep up with all that?" I asked.

"No, by that time he was way behind. We told Wayne to go back with Mr. Anderson because no one was supposed to be alone. The track runner stayed with me. Sometimes when we came to a stream, the dog stopped to get a drink of water, which gave us a chance to catch our breath. Whenever she leaped over precarious places to get to a stream, my friend and I had to jump over too. It was the best jogging exercise either of us ever had!

"Several times we were able to stop and give her another whiff of the bootie. I let the other fellow hold the leash for a while.

"After a long time, Grace found the trail again. She ran along the path all the way, ending up back at the bridge. After crossing it, she began pulling hard, trying to get off the trail. We could see some rabbit holes there. She got onto the pathway again, and followed it all the way to the parking lot.

"Mr. Anderson and Wayne were waiting there for us. The owner was sure Grace had been on Scott's scent, and that Scott was out there somewhere. She had done well, but for some reason hadn't found him. So we thanked Mr. Anderson politely, and he left.

"While we were still there, three horses with riders came plodding into the parking lot. They were relatives of Rick's and had been out since dawn, riding their horses to distant spots. They came to the conclusion that Scott had drowned trying to help the boy who was stuck on the rock, and said that they would not look any more. As they were putting their horses into the trailers, we said 'thank you' for all their efforts, and we told them about our adventures with Grace.

"'We saw quite a few deer out there,' one of the men said. Wayne and I never thought of deer. The trails that Grace followed did look like deer trails, and the matting under the trees were exactly as a deer would make. We were convinced, then, that we had been following deer trails all day!"

Donald had no more to say.

Must our efforts stop here? Should we agree with the horse riders? I was quite disturbed. I didn't want to quit.

Finally I ventured a suggestion: "Are you going to take the dog again? Maybe Grace will catch onto the right trail tomorrow. You should give her another try, don't you think?" I stared at Donald hopefully, terribly frightened that he would say "no."

Mary Jane Warkentin

He paused several minutes and thought deeply. Our son really did believe Grace was a good dog, and that if his brother's scent was in the area recently, she would pick it up—unless the rain washed everything away. Then all would be useless. Yet it would be worth a try. The dog had no known experience of finding a lost person, but Mr. Anderson was thoroughly convinced that she had done it for her previous owner. Actually they had not really gone very close to the turbulent main river that day. Maybe there was more to do.

I waited patiently for Donald to think it all through. At last, he answered, "I suppose we could take her to another place where no dog has been, but I have already told the owner that we were finished with his bloodhound."

"Mr. Anderson said he was very happy for you to use Grace," I hastened to say confidently. "I'll be glad to call him for you, if you care to give it another whirl."

I held my breath while Donald thought it over some more. "All right," he answered, "if we can take her to very remote places—far from where anyone has been searching. I know she can follow a trail. If there is any human scent there, it will have to be Scott's." It would certainly be worth the effort.

Mr. Anderson was delighted that the family had confidence in Grace and wanted to use her again. It would be his pleasure to bring the pet to Fresno, if Donald would return her safely in the evening.

Now the official search in both counties was over. I had to keep reminding myself, and try to be resigned to the thought.

"It's hard to believe how good they have all been to us. And we'll never forget it!" Then I added, "But I am also glad that Grace will be in there again. It's not the end yet! Mr. Anderson's generosity and optimism provided a real comfort at a crucial time when all hope seemed gone and the family needed encouragement.

11

THERE'S AN EMPTINESS INSIDE

Mr. Anderson arrived with Grace early the next morning. Joel, Wayne, Donald, the track champion, and a neighbor boarded our van with the female bloodhound, who weighed a little under a hundred pounds. Before they left, I put my hands on the head of the dog and prayed: "Lord, I commit this animal to You today, especially her nose. Make it sharp in smelling. If it is possible for her to locate Scott, wherever he is, lead her that way. And I do thank You so much. Amen." I never was more sincere in all my life.

They were off. The bulky, reddish brute wandered in a disorderly manner inside the van, drooling on the windows and emitting quite a pungent odor herself.

I was alone. It was an unusual Sunday for Joel and me. We always attended church together, not out of obligation, but because it was encouraging and uplifting. It helped keep our spiritual lives healthy and vibrant.

This Sunday was different. It had been a week now since Scott vanished on that lovely Sunday afternoon in one of the most gorgeous spots of nature I have ever seen. Why should I stay home alone today? What better place could I be than with my understanding Christian friends?

So I prepared to go to church.

To my surprise, things were different there too. Search parties were being formed among the students who were coming to Sunday School. I thought everyone had given up except our family and the dog. Yet it seemed that the search was still going strong! The entire high school department – boys and girls—had already left for the mountains. Adults were getting ready to go. "If Scott is still alive somewhere, or even if he isn't, every effort will be made to locate our fellow Sunday School class member," they told me. "By now he may be delirious or in a stupor.

Whatever his condition, there is no time for delay, even if it is Sunday."

I continued to cling to the more comforting thought that he must be surviving on plants and existing somehow. "Why does he have to be half dead, just because he is lost?" I reasoned.

When the church service began—with a smaller crowd—the minister said, "Scott Warkentin is absent from us this morning—blond, quiet Scott Warkentin—your friend and mine. That leaves us with many questions, and a sense of emptiness. Has Scott gone to be with the Lord? Is Scott waiting for us to find him? Is he okay? Or is he not? We think about Scott, and our sense of compassion reaches out beyond him to Joel, to Mary Jane, and to the family. We find ourselves with them simply trusting, and waiting, and praying, and caring, and loving."

As I listened, tears flowed gently down my cheeks. Not wanting to leave, I kept wiping my face with a tissue. I blew my nose softly.

The choir members had told me what an inspiration Scott was to them. He always sat in the second pew by himself, following the Scriptures in his big Bible, and listening intently to the preacher's message. One soprano admitted that she often peeked during the prayers so she could be inspired by watching him in his devout worship as he communed with God. I wondered if Scott would be back in his place to help the singers do their best next Sunday.

The minister continued, "In times like these we feel so strongly our sense of limitation. And so we long for the source of strength that we need. We long for the reality of God's presence with Scott, with the Warkentins, and with us.

"Scott is not alone. Wherever he is at this moment, he is not alone. Neither are Joel nor Mary Jane, nor the rest of the family. Neither are we; we have the presence of God with us.

"Although we sorrow and have questions, we know the Holy Spirit can fill our emptiness. This very week Mary Jane, even while they searched for Scott, felt moved to teach her Bible study at Evangel Home. And do you know what happened? The

Lost, But Not Forever

Holy Spirit spoke through her and transcended every expectation. A woman came to know Jesus Christ as her personal Saviour!

"That same Holy Spirit can come to you in your personal need, your personal limitation, today, right now. There is only one real answer to fill that emptiness, and it is to make room for the Spirit of God to enter in and to take control. Our prayers, Mary Jane and Joel, are that this fulness of the Holy Spirit will invade your lives anew today, and that as a church we will let Him come in and lead us where He wants us to go."

When the service was over, friends gathered around me to express their love and concern with affection and many kind words. I felt exhilarated at the same time that my inner being was plagued with pain. God was showing His love and His gentle care through these people, and I appreciated it. Truly it did lighten my burden.

However, I was upset later about a comment the minister made to me after church. He wanted to come to our house for a visit during the week.

"He has a memorial service in mind," I feared, shrinking from such a thought. "I'm not ready for a memorial service! I don't want one! They may give up the search after today, but how do we know he's dead? I don't think he is."

Finally I confronted the minister and told him what I was thinking. He had no such thought, but only wanted to help in whatever way he could.

Joel had decided to investigate with his group along some of the smaller roads. The map showed a likely turn-off from the main road at an old cemetery, but they were having a hard time finding it. Stopping to ask a storekeeper, they were given directions to a firefighter who lived nearby and who knew every dirt road in the vicinity.

They found him getting ready to burn brush, but he willingly stopped what he was doing to talk. Donald stayed with the dog near the van.

Mary Jane Warkentin

"Do you have a son named Ralph?" he asked.

"Yes."

"He was here yesterday looking for his brother." It seemed that wherever they went, Scott's "buddy" had already been there. The firefighter and his wife spent an hour explaining what they knew about the behavior and thinking of lost persons. For instance, he said our son might be pinched between two rocks unable to move. Or he could have received a blow on the head and might be in a state of amnesia—walking back and forth, or going in circles without realizing it. The man was very methodical, with helpful suggestions.

He informed them that it was seven miles to one lake and fourteen miles to another from Squaw Leap. In a week Scott should have reached one or the other, if he were walking along the river. The fire captain outlined distances to various places. Scott would have reached one of them by now, regardless of the direction he was walking. By following any one of numerous roads he would have reached some kind of civilization—a ranch house, store, or something. His wife told of a cabin with provisions in it that was kept by a prospector near an old mining mill at Titcomb Flat.

Before they left, the firefighter mentioned a cattleman and gave them directions to his twelve-thousand-acre ranch.

Joel and the others took his advice and drove to the ranch. The cattleman was immediately receptive and wanted to help in every way he could. He was a salty, seventy-year-old character, who seemingly had a soft heart. After inviting them into his house, he told them of possible places to look on his land. He pulled out a large map of his property and described various features in detail, spending considerable time with them. He said he would very much like to go with them, but could not because of other pressing business that day.

"Here's a ring of keys," he said. "These will open all the locked gates on my ranch. Look wherever you need to. I'll loan you this map too. It's valuable, so hang onto it; guard it with your life! It shows every detail of my property. Stay as long as

Lost, But Not Forever

you like, and I hope you find what you're looking for." They were amazed at his generosity and thanked him heartily.

As soon as they were back on the road, Joel stated excitedly, "I'm going to go to Titcomb Flat where that stocked cabin is!" He headed his vehicle in that direction, his hope renewed, and he told the others in the van, "We are going to that cabin to get Scott!" I believe he meant it! His anticipation ran high as they approached the old ore milling works at Titcomb Flat.

Sure enough, among the several buildings in odd stages of decay stood a cabin that was quite secure-looking. They all got out to investigate. Joel's sister had repeatedly expressed the strong intuition that Scott was staying in a cabin somewhere. Here it was—Scott must be safe and secure inside. Anxiously Joel quickened his pace as he approached the shack, the others trudging along behind.

He found the doors locked and the windows all in place. He looked inside and all around. Scott was not there.

A good supply of wood was stacked against the wall. There were provisions, including plenty of food. Pieces of iron and pipe were lying nearby that one could use to force his way inside, in case of emergency. Surely Scott could have survived here for at least a week in a reasonable state of comfort.

But his son was not there. This time Joel had expected to find Scott, because of the premonition. A feeling of high hopes faded. Where else could Scott be? He must just not be alive any more. Before leaving, they examined each of the other buildings inch by inch. Then sadly, Joel turned the van around and started back down the rough dirt road, pocked with mud holes and slippery stretches.

After a few miles, they stopped for a trek down to the river. The big bloodhound was given a good noseful of Scott's bootie, then went with them. The hike down Grapevine Canyon revealed extremely rugged terrain. There was a good-sized creek running through the canyon, and the sides were profusely abundant with wild flowers, including many California poppies.

Mary Jane Warkentin

A deer leaped across the trail just ahead. "Oh no," thought Donald, "Grace is going to go crazy when she has to pass that spot." But the dog didn't even seem to smell the deer tracks; she made no reaction at all.

Everybody called, "Scott, Scott," as they went along. Joel had a whistle and blew it periodically.

The foot of the canyon took them to a place in the river called Patterson Bend. They could look far down-stream and also upstream—no sign of any human activity. Whenever they came to an empty building, it was checked methodically to see if Scott might be there; but all were empty.

The group stayed on the twelve-thousand-acre ranch until dusk. At the end of the day they returned to the cattleman's home to bring back the map and keys. A friend was visiting him. "In the thirty years I've lived around here," he said, "no one has ever made it along the river past those canyons. The terrain is just too rough."

So the weekend was over, and Grace was returned to her owner. I even had a moment of laughter when I found a note I had written beside the telephone. I had been talking to Mr. Anderson about using the dog, and he was describing to me how Grace functioned differently from other search dogs—needing to sniff a piece of the lost person's clothing. I had written on a piece of scratch paper by the telephone, not realizing how funny it sounded. The note read: THIS DOG HAS TO HAVE CLOTHES.

12

IT WAS LIKE A SANDWICH

Folks were always asking Joel and me, "How are you doing?" We had the feeling that people were not merely giving a greeting, but were probing for a sincere answer. Sometimes I would say, "I know my son is lost in the mountains, but at the same time thousands of people are praying for me."

It certainly was a mixed feeling. The prayers could definitely be felt. As the Bible says, "The peace of God, which passeth all understanding, shall keep your hearts and minds through Christ Jesus" (Philippians 4:7). There is no way to explain that peace. It truly is a "peace that passes understanding."

Joel and I found God's hand to be evident in many ways during those days. For one thing, the tragedy of our missing son was timed perfectly. It was sandwiched in between one of the happiest weeks of my life and a very refreshing visit with my seldom-seen brother.

The week before Scott's disappearance was a time of deep joy for me—a spiritual high, you might say. More prayers than usual were being answered. Friends who had strayed were coming back to the Lord and getting into church again. I was just plain happy! Was God preparing me for the week ahead? Surely He wanted me to pass the test I was soon to undergo.

Besides that, it had been prearranged a few months ago that I would meet my brother from Ohio, Walter, for a two-day stay in San Francisco. The date happened to fall during the week after Scott's disappearance.

Joel said, "This is just what you need right now. There can be no better therapy for you at this time than a visit with Walter. He always knows how to say the right thing at the right time."

Walter was chairman of the mechanical engineering department at Ohio State University. What interested me most

Mary Jane Warkentin

was his sideline—he was an expert on "freak accidents". If a mishap occurred, Walter was often consulted for an opinion on the possible cause of the accident. He often testified in court for large corporations, So I boarded a plane for San Francisco after Scott's "freak accident" to be with a freak-accident specialist! Studying the panorama below from the airplane window, I mused on what Walter's opinion might be. I expected him to say almost anything.

He was waiting at the airport for me. It was so good to see him! After claiming my baggage, Walter said, "Come and let's sit over here. I have something amusing to tell you."

We found a secluded spot some distance from the milling crowds and sat down. "As I wrote in my letter," my brother began, "I will be staying in one of San Francisco's finest hotels while I am here. It so happens that one of the big shots at the conference has the same last name as mine. His name is Donald Starkey. So, when I registered for my room last night, they apparently thought I was he, and I was given one of the largest and most tastefully decorated rooms in the hotel." He grinned broadly as he chuckled, "You should see how elegant it is! I had no idea why I was given such a room. Then, in the middle of the evening a hotel employee knocked on my door and walked in with a huge bowl filled with many varieties of fruits, crackers, olives, and what-not.

"'My!' I said, 'Do you treat all your guests like this?'

"He said, 'No, just special ones; this is for Mr. Starkey.'

"I answered, 'Well, I'm Mr. Starkey, but there must be some mistake.'"

"I suppose you got to keep all the goodies?" I asked, wide-eyed.

"No," he laughed, "when he learned of the mistaken identity, he took them away. It was fun while it lasted."

Then Walter looked serious, and facing me said, "Mary Jane, what do you think happened to Scott?"

"I have no idea," I told him sincerely. So we talked about the massive and thorough search which had been carried on by

Lost, But Not Forever

Fresno and Madera Counties and by so many volunteers, what a wonderful attitude everyone had, and how determined they were in their efforts. Walter listened intently, and the burden seemed to lift somewhat as I talked.

We had supper in a quaint little restaurant near the hotel. Since I was very anxious to hear my brother's expert opinion on what he thought might have happened to Scott, I said as we were eating, "Walter, I'd like to tell you more of the details of Scott's disappearance. I want you to think it over and see if you can tell me what might have happened to him. Why can't we find him?"

"That's fine," said Walter. "I would be glad to hear it, but I already know what I think happened to Scott."

"You do?" I was a bit surprised. "What?"

"I think he drowned in the river," he answered simply, with conviction.

"You do?" It was like a bomb shell—an awful let-down feeling. The pain that was always there in my stomach suddenly felt worse. "What makes you so sure?"

"It's the only place he could be. If the search was as extensive as you say, he couldn't be anywhere else or he would have been found."

It sounded convincing...my hopes sank...no, I rebelled, "But Scott could have been kidnapped, or maybe he walked out of the searched area, or was eaten by a wild animal. He could even have been translated by God into heaven—it happened to Enoch." (See Genesis 5:24.) I argued hard, but was Walter right?

"I believe it happened right away before any of the search began," Walter continued. "I don't think he was ever lost or that he suffered for more than a few seconds. Drowning is one of the most painless deaths there is, you know," Walter reassured me.

I winced, then considered it carefully. After all, the hardest part for us had been not knowing where Scott was and if he were hurting. I recalled one time I had even told God, "Oh, if Scott's body were only safe in a coffin and his soul in heaven!" I really wasn't sure that was what I wanted.

I thought of all this. But now Walter said he was dead! And Walter was one of the country's top experts on freak accidents. I did feel a certain relief in believing that Scott had not suffered and that it was all over.

Walter explained further, "You see, the way you have described that terrain near the river, it must be very wild country. Am I right?"

I nodded.

"He may have approached the river to get a closer look, as boys will do. He could hear the river and knew it was nearby, but didn't realize he was so close, because of the thick underbrush. He could step right over the brink without realizing it. It's so easy to do."

"That's probably true," I admitted slowly, trying hard to resign myself to such a thought. "And besides," I added, "because of the downpours we've been having, the rocks are very shaky. So much dirt has eroded from under them. Scott could have stepped on a loose rock, thinking it would hold him."

"Exactly," said my brother.

"That did actually happen to Donald's friend," I recalled, referring to the track runner. "He had not even been very near the surface of the water, but way on top near the brink. The young man slipped off a large rock that gave way under him while he was looking for Scott. If he had not managed to catch a branch, he would have fallen down the cliff about a hundred feet into the river. Joel also stepped on a very large rock that seemed secure." I gestured to show Walter just how big it was. "It rolled under him and actually knocked him down."

All was quiet as we both sat there in meditation. It didn't matter that our food was getting cold. I had acknowledged this all along as a strong possibility, but there seemed to be a finality about it now. This was a solemn moment for me. Somehow, in the midst of it, I loved God very much...and heaven seemed closer to me than it ever had before.

Lost, But Not Forever

The next morning in that elegantly decorated hotel room, I took out my Bible to have a bit of devotional time before beginning the day. I opened the book to Romans, because that was where Scott's youth group had been studying on Wednesday nights at the church.

Before reading, I began to contemplate the events of one evening not too long ago when I drove Scott to church to meet with the other young people. I had asked him, "Que estudian ustedes esta noche?" or "What are you studying tonight?" He had begun learning Spanish in school and I knew he liked to speak it with me. I still remembered some Spanish from my high school days, so he enjoyed testing me on his new words and to learn others from me. I was amazed how well he could speak Spanish with the accent of a true Mexican!

"Estudiamos Romanos, un libro de la Biblia," he had replied, sounding so much better than I did. He had told me that they were studying Romans, a book of the Bible.

"Romanos habla del pecado y los pecadores," or "Romans speaks of sins and sinners," I had commented. I was glad the Spanish words I knew matched what I wanted to say.

Scott liked a good Bible study. He didn't care to fool around when the kids got together. He knew his Bible well, and now he was taking a keen interest in languages. He was blessed with a terrific memory, and he seemed to absorb new words like a sponge without having to make a conscious effort to memorize them. He even found pleasure in reading the "foreign word derivatives" section of the dictionary. He was fascinated by anything he could learn of any language.

If he keeps on this way, he could be a Bible translator when he grew up. It would be great to decipher the unwritten language of some primitive tribe and record it on paper. Or he would be good at translating the Bible into a new language so that people could read the Bible who had never been able to before. I had been so excited about the idea and had wanted to suggest it to him. He was only fifteen, but it was not too soon to make plans for the future. His school counselor had told me that he wanted to be a writer, so that was certainly a step in that direction.

Should I mention the idea of being a Bible translator to him? No, if God wants Scott to do that, God Himself will let him know, I had told myself.

When God calls someone for His service, there is no mistaking it. He makes it very plain. There may not be an audible voice, but a strong undeniable urge will persist until its meaning is hard to dispute. So I had never mentioned all this to Scott.

Now, as I sat in the hotel room, I looked at the book of Romans. Walter was reading a magazine, seated comfortably in an overstuffed chair across the room.

It suddenly hit me—does all this mean that Scott can never be a Bible translator? I had been so excited about such a prospect, and now it all seemed to crumble at my feet. I couldn't stop the tears that began to pour down my face.

"What's the matter?" asked Walter, noticing my dilemma.

I couldn't tell him. "I was just going to read Romans in the Bible because that is what Scott was studying in church," I answered sniffling.

Tears turned into uncontrollable sobs.

All Walter could gently say was, "Bless you."

Our time in San Francisco passed all too quickly. Walter and I chatted in plush hotel lobbies. We rode the world-famous cable cars and toured the Maritime Museum. Such fun it was to devour scrumptious ice cream at the Chocolate Factory in Ghirardeli Square, and then walk all the long way back to the hotel up San Francisco's notoriously steep streets to burn off the calories! There was always so much to talk about. Lighthearted laughter helped ease my broken heart. Serious discussions served to give me new direction and hope.

Then Walter left.

At the airport I was waiting for my homeward-bound plane—to go back to a partially vacated house and try to live

Lost, But Not Forever

with the thought that our son's body was somewhere wedged under a rock deep within the churning San Joaquin River, and that we would never know what really happened. I was sure that God knew, and I would have to be content with that.

Deciding to use my time in the airport to write thank-you notes, I composed a letter to the editor of our local newspaper:

> We wish to express our appreciation to all of the good people who came to our aid or felt a concern in a time of need.
>
> When we lost our fifteen-year-old son, Scott Warkentin, at Squaw Leap above Millerton Lake on April 2, we received immediate response from official agencies and volunteers. There was no hesitation in providing help such as airplanes, helicopter, rock climbers, dogs, posses and ground crews. Every effort was made at personal risk through very unpleasant conditions. Many took off work at their own expense to search. Friends and neighbors provided food for the searchers and family. Others showed their love and concern with phone calls, visits, cards, and letters. We believe thousands of people must have been praying.
>
> We wish to thank each person who cared about us during this most difficult time in our lives. So much kindness has been bestowed upon us. It makes us feel so good.
>
> Although we still do not know what happened to Scott, we go on with renewed faith in a good God and in the kindness of humanity, surrounded by the love of many friends.
>
> > Joel and Mary Jane Warkentin
> > and family

There...that seemed to wind up everything.

Mary Jane Warkentin

I began to look around the airport. The surging crowds milled about, some aimlessly passing the time, and others intent on getting somewhere.

Two Moonies were busy in the center of the throbbing lounge, approaching one after another with "ma'am" or "sir." Most people brushed them aside, not lingering long enough to hear what these followers of a South Korean "messiah" might have to say. The girls' vitality and undaunted spirit amazed me. Occasionally someone would listen a bit and press a coin into one of the girls' hand.

Shall I listen or walk by? I would be passing that way soon. As I thought about it, the time approached when I had to find my way to Gate 8, where my plane would be boarding.

"I'll do neither," I decided with determination. "I have something to say, and I want to share it with this girl." I picked up my bag and walked up to one of the Moonies.

"Hello," I began confidently. Surprised, the girl turned toward me.

"I have just found out that my son may have fallen into the river and drowned; but I want you to know that my God is sufficient, and that I wouldn't trade Him for anything else in the world."

"We are theology students," was the young girl's answer. "Could you give us a contribution to help others have as strong a faith in God as you have?"

"I give my offering other places, but if you will take Jesus as your Savior"—I put my hand on the girl's shoulder—"then you will have great joy in anything and everything. God bless you."

I just had to say it.

The girl looked baffled, and shrugged her shoulders as I walked off to board my plane for home.

I was glad that I hadn't passed her by.

13

JUST IN TIME FOR THE DRESS PARADE

No sooner had I arrived home from San Francisco than our local T.V. channel came to interview me for the evening news. I spoke of my visit with my brother, and that the only conclusion Walter could come to was that Scott had fallen into the river.

Later we celebrated Ralph's nineteenth birthday. Our family always observed special days with a get-together, complete with cake, ice cream and presents. When the children were little, I often prepared a treasure hunt with the presents being the reward at the end of the hunt. As they grew older, Scott liked continuing this practice, and he usually prepared and hid papers that read, "Look under Donald's bed," or "Look behind the piano." He had enough fun-loving boyishness in him that, if Scott had been there, a treasure hunt might still have been part of the celebration.

Renetta had baked and decorated one of her delicious cakes for the occasion. Ralph's one big breath was enough to blow out all the candles. Even though it was under dire and unusual circumstances, with Scott having been gone for two weeks, it was nice for the family to be together for a time of enjoyment.

As I tried to return to my usual household duties, I found that the telephone was playing an increasing role. If it weren't ringing, I knew it would soon. Calls were coming in from everywhere—local and long distance. Most phone calls were from well-wishers who wanted us to know that they cared and that they were praying for us.

People felt helpless—not knowing what to do. They didn't need to do anything—just assuring us that they were concerned was enough. Their words of comfort were greatly appreciated, and the sincere expression of each one's desire to help was like a soothing salve. Each was fulfilling in his own way the Bible verse that says, "They helped every one his neighbor; and everyone said to his brother, be of good courage" (Isaiah 41:6). Their expressions of concern lifted our spirits, in spite of our uneasiness and the big empty hole that continued to nag in the pit of our stomachs.

One thing I didn't like, however, was silence. For many years I didn't know what to say to a person who had experienced a misfortune in his life. I did the worst thing possible—I would avoid the individual because I didn't know what to say and I felt awkward about it. For a certain period of time I tried to keep my distance and say nothing. How immature! I am glad that most people had more sense than that in dealing with us. I liked for them to talk about what had happened. I didn't mind frankness; I wanted to talk about Scott—anything about him, openly. But I didn't like it when someone discussed everything except Scott. After all, he was the one on my mind and I knew that they were thinking of him too, so why be silent? I've decided it's better to talk about the cause of the sadness than to avoid the subject for fear of saying the wrong thing.

There is, however, one exception. What we didn't need at that time was the lengthy, gruesome story of someone else's tragic experience. Just to mention a personal difficulty casually was tolerable; but when a friend began telling us about another tragedy, we always hoped he wouldn't go into any detail. Our own disaster was all we were able to handle at that time, and then only by the grace of God. Yet this did seem to be a common occurence and it was hard for us to take.

Some found helpful ways to show their concern by bringing a plant or a consoling cassette tape. One friend painted a plaque for the family.

Even though Walter believed Scott had drowned, limited searches continued, but not with the same intensity as before. Now it was mostly that they hoped to find a dead body.

Three men, separately, had taken boats to Millerton Lake and voyaged part way up the river, until the velocity and turbulence of the water stopped them.

Lost, But Not Forever

One of these, a neighbor, was most anxious to go as far up the river in his boat as he could. When he had first heard of Scott's disappearance, he'd had an immediate compulsion to go and search for him. He had hiked along the river a few times before, but decided he needed to take his boat.

He and his brother-in-law launched the boat into Millerton Lake and headed toward the mouth of the river, which was about five miles downstream from where Scott had disappeared. The day was balmy and the water near the lake was clear and calm. They had come there often to go fishing, but that day there was more important business at hand. The neighbor had known Scott since he was a baby, and their boys had played ball together through the years. He felt that Scott, or his body, must be found.

As they headed up the river, they kept their eyes open for the log jam located at the point where the cold water of the river meets the warmer water of the lake, which can vary as much as a half-mile up or down stream, according to the amount of water in the river at the time. Some such mass—consisting of sticks, brush, logs, and other debris carried downstream by the river is always there somewhere. The head of the forest service had told them that two boats should always go together, in case one of the propellers was disabled by an underwater log.

Before long they spotted the filmy, dirty-looking debri-filled water. They didn't have time to decide whether they should proceed slowly and cautiously, or just barge ahead full speed and hope for the best. Before they could hardly think, they saw a large boat coming downsteam which quickly plunged headlong through the log jam as if it weren't even there at all! Our neighbor accelerated into the path left by the other larger boat and they went right through the jam.

They continued travelling up the river, but not for long. The rapids loomed ahead, and they could see the white water forming. Soon they were forced by the current to tie up the boat and continue by land. That wasn't easy either. As soon as they stepped from the boat, one man sank into the sand to the calves

Mary Jane Warkentin

and the other up to his thighs! Yet they managed to struggle out and plod on toward the cliff.

Vultures were flying overhead, but the men knew that as long as the birds were just circling, their presence wasn't significant. After they had trudged along some distance, however, one vulture suddenly swooped to the ground and didn't come back up. Our neighbor felt a sinking feeling in his stomach as he quickened his pace toward the spot, but it seemed to recede into the distance like a mirage on the desert. Time was growing short, and he knew the place where the vulture had landed was too distant for him to reach and still have time to get back into town for his two daughters' fashion show, or "dress parade" as he called it. Reluctantly, they were forced to give up the quest.

On their return trip through the log jam they did hit wood, and one big log popped up out of the water as the propeller chopped on it. But they plowed on through the heavy debris without hurting the boat. And they did make it home in time to see the two girls each win a prize at the "dress parade."

Our neighbor woke up nights after that, thinking about that experience and wishing that he'd had more time to investigate. He kept wondering whether the vulture swooping to the ground had meant anything. Maybe Scott's body was indeed there.

Ralph kept asking his dad why a more comprehensive search for Scott's body was not continuing. Joel replied that every possible place had been investigated. Ralph thought otherwise. He said there were numerous places that had not been checked, and he wanted to find good hikers who would go out into a wider area to explore. Ralph often encouraged the family to keep on looking, even though we thought the search was over. Ralph and Scott were the two youngest and always had been very close friends.

So Joel made some calls, and several college students who were good rock climbers agreed to go with Ralph. They hiked along the river all the way to the lake.

Then Rick decided to take off again from work and go with Ralph. They started from Powerhouse Road north of Kerckoff Lake and worked their way into the wilderness. Then down they trudged into Mike Walker Canyon, and hiked along the canyon to near its confluence with the San Joaquin River, across Kerchoff Dam to Powerhouse Road. The two of them returned home, having looked behind many a bush, rock, or hidden spot. They were bushed!

Over two weeks had gone by since Scott had last been seen. Every ravine and rock formation in the vicinity had surely by now been searched. Maps of the area, which by then were sold out in the local sporting goods stores, were getting worn from much study and strategy planning.

Another weekend arrived, and Joel decided that he would like to go up and circle the entire Squaw Leap perimeter in his van. "I'll show you what the countryside up there looks like," he said to me. "It may do you good to get out. We can take a lunch along and make a little outing of it, stop at Renetta's along the way, if you like."

It was a rainy, squalid day—not a good day to stay home and feel morbid anyway. I hadn't been back near that region since the day of the picnic.

Before passing through town, we neared a shopping center. "There's a sale going on over there," Joel noticed. "Is there anything you want?" I looked as he pointed to a fashionable department store. He knew I had a woman's desire for a bargain.

"You mean it?" He usually wasn't that anxious for me to spend money, but it would be nice to look around.

"Let's go see what they have," he decided for me. It was the first time since Scott's disappearance that we had done anything we didn't have to do. That day we were going to be together and do something for ourselves.

Once inside the store, it didn't take long to glance past several attractions and find a pink pantsuit that especially caught my fancy. When I slipped it on, the garment fit perfectly.

Mary Jane Warkentin

"Go ahead and get it, if you like," Joel encouraged me. I wouldn't argue with that! "Just a little thing to cheer you up during these trying days," he said.

Back in the van, we set off again toward the Sierra foothills. It was nice to be together in a relaxed sort of way.

It was a pleasant drive to the hills, then we took the main roads that circled Squaw Leap. It was encouraging to me, after hearing so much about the wildness of the river area, to see the many ranch houses and other evidences of civilization not too far out from Squaw Leap. Certainly Scott—if he had not drowned in the river as Walter said—could have gone to any of them for help. The people there would have taken him home, or at least informed someone where he was. All the way we kept our eyes open for a six-foot, blond hitch-hiker—just in case.

By mealtime the rain was pouring hard. We found a picturesque spot and parked along the road to eat the lunch we had packed. It was a cozy picnic—the two of us munching sandwiches while the rain splashed and splattered all over the windows of the van.

When we reached Renetta's, the downpour had subsided enough that we could dash inside without getting too wet. We found her alone with her baby, Matthew. Renetta was a pretty young lady. She looked much younger than twenty-four, with a slim waist and long, flowing light brown hair. All the children had begun as blonds, like their father, but had deepened into varying shades of brown.

Rick, Ralph, and the foster daughters were still out looking for Scott when we arrived. After we had visited for some time in the spacious living room around the immense stone fireplace, the gang arrived home wet and tired.

"Cindi fell in the mud," Ralph told us. "I thought it was quicksand. She began sinking deeper and deeper, and I knew I'd better rescue her. So I tried to pull her out, but it didn't work so well." Cindi was one of Renetta's foster daughters.

"Yeah, you sank in the mud deeper than I did!" said Cindi, chuckling.

Lost, But Not Forever

"Well, I'm glad you both made it back okay," Renetta laughed.

After a satisfying visit, Joel and I drove home. As we reached the front door, the phone was ringing. It was someone from the church.

"The ladies want to bring dinners to you, starting tomorrow night. Will it be all right?"

"Oh, you don't need to do that," I told her. "Eating really isn't very important to us right now. We appreciate your kindness, but there is no need to go to all that bother. We'll just open cans; that's fine. Thanks so much."

"Please let the ladies do it," she insisted. "They really want to. They are anxious to do something more for you and your family." Up until then women from the church had been preparing and sending food to Squaw Leap for the searchers. Neighbors and friends had also been bringing food to us.

"Okay then," I agreed, realizing this was an outlet for women who cared and wanted to show their concern.

So each evening for nearly two weeks different ladies from the church rang our doorbell about supper time and carried in steaming bowls of appetizing meals. They usually stayed a while to talk. It was a real expression of love, and it surely did beat opening cans!

One evening—after one of those good dinners—Joel, Donald, and I were sitting in the family room. As always, Scott was much on our minds. It was still hard to even talk of other things, and we didn't try.

"Scott was so excited about that waterfall on the other side of the river," Joel began.

"I'm sure he was. All the searchers were talking about it—really very picturesque," Donald put in.

"What waterfall?" I felt left out and quite curious.

"The one he wanted me to see on the way back." said Joel.

Mary Jane Warkentin

"Wait a minute," I insisted, "I know there were little streams and falls all over the place, but I never heard of any one special waterfall that Scott liked. Tell me more."

"This incident just hasn't crossed my mind until now," Joel confessed. "Well, as Scott and I were hustling along the path toward the river that first day, he ran on ahead of me. In a few minutes he was back to tell me about a large, rushing waterfall that he had seen on the other side of the river. I hadn't noticed it, but I said I'd be sure to look for it on the way back up."

"Did you?"

"Yes, I did."

"Was it pretty?"

"Very pretty. Didn't you see it?"

"I don't remember seeing any thing like that."

All at once something struck me. "Joel!" I exclaimed. "If Scott spotted a waterfall over there on the other side of the river, of course that's where he would go! That's why he wanted to go over there and didn't even wait for you to go with him when you stopped to take pictures of the river. He absolutely loves waterfalls! If I had been along, we would both have gone to see it. You never told me about this in all these two weeks."

I was sure that I had the answer. He'd left the trail to find the waterfall and had gotten too close. How excited he must have been about that huge waterfall.

"Did it lead into the river about there?" I almost whispered.

"I'm sure it did," was Donald's reply.

All was quiet.

14

EVERYONE HELPED HIS NEIGHBOR

Life as usual? Back to the routine? Was it possible? It had to be. Scott had drowned in the river—so everyone thought—and I tried to accept it. But as hard as I tried, I couldn't keep my mind from wandering. What if Scott were still alive somewhere? It was possible, no matter what anyone said!

I thought back to that first day at Squaw Leap. Maybe he did find his way back to the parking lot without our seeing him. Scott might have explored that road down where the target practice was going on. A stray bullet could have injured or killed him. Could the gunman have taken his body away to dispose of the evidence?

A wild idea—but did Bigfoot get him? Or perhaps a spaceship? I thought of everything! There seemed to be no sense to the idea of his being kidnapped, but senseless deeds and senseless people are all over, possibly even on nature trails. A few folks suggested that he might have run away, but only strangers said this—those who did not know Scott's nature or his strong love for his home and family.

What about the young fellow we met beside the road as we drove up to Squaw Leap the day of the picnic? His van was stuck in a steep, rutted incline a few miles below the parking lot. He had tried and failed to make it up a small dirt road. Although Joel knew he couldn't pull the man's van out with his station wagon, he stopped and offered to help if there were anything he could do. We had no idea what kind of person he was, but the man got into our car, hoping to find a willing hand with a jeep farther up the road. At the parking lot we let him out, wished him well, and never saw him again. He had been sitting beside Scott in the back seat. My mind reflected on this, as I imagined what could have happened.

Mary Jane Warkentin

"Hey kid," he might have yelled to Scott when we were out of sight. "I'm getting a ride down the hill in that jeep over there. Will you come along and help get my van loose? We'll give you a ride back up." Scott would have wanted to help; could they have done something sinister to him?

Days went by, yet the unknown fact of what really happened to our young son would not stay buried in our souls. It seemed to plague us all, and many friends continued to do what they could to help.

For instance, a customer of Ralph's contributed three day's pay to enable him to take more time from work to look for Scott. This man also drove his motorhome to the upper end of the lake twice, and left the search-light on all night as a guide, in case Scott were still nearby and might come that way. Every once in a while— about every hour— he honked his horn loudly during the night. Other friends, who owned airplanes, flew over the entire countryside hoping to spot our son. Every time we thought the case to be closed someone felt inspired anew to do some more. After all, Scott's body, or his clothes at least, had to exist somewhere.

Dave Graves, who had put himself in charge of soliciting and organizing workers from the church, was continuing to leave his job as often as he possibly could, to search for remaining clues. One Sunday he took a recess, because he felt that he should spend some time with his wife and two babies (one a newborn). She had patiently released him, and as a result had seen very little of her husband, even on weekends. She told me, "Dave felt guilty for taking time away from looking for Scott to be with us. He feels that he has done so little. What a strong urge he has to help all he can!" Actually it was unbelievable how much he had done!

Another youth had been living at the coast when he heard about Scott's predicament. He had injured his back at work, but he could walk in the mountains, so he moved nearby and was going up practically every day, even though he had never seen Scott and didn't even know our family previously. Such

Lost, But Not Forever

willingness and dedication by so many noble souls was mind-boggling to us. Our heart nearly exploded in grateful appreciation! This dedicated young man also became a member of our church staff. So Scott's disappearance was working for good by leading someone into active service in the church. The lad settled down in this area, and has become a leader of Scott's group—the high school people. It is inspiring to see how well he has developed his leadership abilities.

One teacher had used up all his emergency leave on our project. He explained the situation at his school, saying, "The thing that impressed me the most was the willingness and cooperation of the people who participated in the search. It was a real test of their strength. Some helped for a day or two, but their legs, knees, and ankles became so bruised they were unable to continue. Others worked day after day, whenever they could be free. Even though those who were there did not know Scott very well, or at all, they still did what they could. There was no question in anybody's mind but that we were going to find him. Another thing that impressed me was the number of people—both staff and parents—who asked and were interested for days and weeks afterward. The number of individuals the experience reached was just astronomical!"

Everything this teacher told us was new to us; we were completely unaware that any of this was going on, because it wasn't someone from Scott's school, or from Joel's school, or that of any of his brothers. It was just a school of big-hearted people who cared.

People were still visiting us in our home, although less frequently now. Visits and phone calls were helpful if they were short, but I had things to do and tired easily. I didn't need anyone to sit with me for lengthy periods, but preferred to be alone much of the time. What we both liked the best were cards and letters. They did just as much as a phone call or visit, and yet we could read them uninterupted in our own time. The mail always contained something to lift our spirits.

One helpful visit to our home was from a minister and his wife who had lost their son in a similar way several years before. He has never been found, yet they demonstrated an inspiring spirit of triumph. How my heart went out to those parents at the time! Their son had been our newspaper boy. He had gone back-packing by himself, and did not return. An enormous search was carried on for him. When time passed, and it looked as if he would not be found, I thought that was one of the worst things I ever heard! My own four sons came to mind, and I wondered how any mother could ever stand it. When I tried to put myself into her shoes, I couldn't do it—the pain was too great.

If anyone had told me that such would be my lot, I would say, "No, not me—never would I be able to take that!" And now people were telling me and my husband that we inspired them by the victory we showed! This could only be God's grace. The Lord provides strength for us if we let Him. It is not our strength, but His!

A lady friend of mine reflected and told me her story. Ann became so discouraged that eventually she gave up—threw in the towel and quit. For six years she did not walk with the Lord. She neglected; she strayed; she no longer cared. When the chance of employment came to her from a questionable business firm, Ann began working there, even though, at a time when her heart was right with God, this would have been against her conscience.

As time went along, the business changed hands and a new boss was soon to arrive. Ann decided to use this occasion as an opportunity to ask for a sign from God. Although she wasn't walking with Him, she could pray.

"If it is Your will that I come back to You," she said simpleheartedly, "then I pray that I may not work here any longer." What a daring sign to ask, in order to prove what she already knew—that her loving Father was not pleased with her lifestyle, and that He was calling her back to Himself!

Lost, But Not Forever

At the same time, she heard a report on the evening news that Scott Warkentin was missing in the mountains. This startled Ann into thinking seriously, and she realized what kind of a reaction she would experience if a similar event should happen unexpectedly to her in such a back-slidden condition. "Mrs. Warkentin is walking with the Lord," Ann told herself, "And this is helping her to endure this awful thing. I am not! I must straighten up my life while there is still time."

God granted Ann's request and she was fired from the objectionable job. "I was glad," was her response, "so happy!" She thanked God for working it all together, and she told Him, "Please, Lord, take me back, and give me the kind of strength You have granted Mrs. Warkentin."

Very soon Ann was invited to my women's Bible study and prayer group, where she has remained and grown in a closer walk with God.

15

MYSTERIOUS SURPRISES

One day I was cleaning Scott's room. We called it the "fish room" now because it housed five aquariums of tropical fish.

As I dust-mopped the floor and my mind wandered aimlessly, I was thinking about the well-wishers who had visited us recently. Many of them wore sad faces. They meant well and were meaning to be sympathetic, but it depressed me.

Mechanically I was moving things about to do a little dusting of the furniture, when my eyes fell upon a full sheet of paper in Scott's handwriting. Curious, I picked it up, and found that it was a letter to someone named "Roger."[1] As I read, I became more fascinated:

---

[1] I have changed his name.

Lost, But Not Forever

Roger,

Hi! You don't know me, but I ask you to still read this letter. I'm Scott. I live in Fresno. I heard about you approximately one year ago. This letter is about salvation from Jesus Christ. Now you may believe that Jesus died close to two thousand years ago. I believe he rose again.

Time and time again I have begun to write to you usually not getting more than a few lines. I have already gotten an envelope and stamped and adressed it. I have not yet, at this writing, mailed anything to you.

When I heard about you, I heard that you were thinking of commiting suicide. My advice to you is this: THAT YOU ACCEPT JESUS CHRIST AS YOUR PERSONAL LORD AND SAVIOUR.

You may think that Christianity is only going to church on Sundays, giving away your money and obeying rules. Only when one becomes a mature Christian do they realize that that myth is totally wrong. To the mature Christian, Christianity is great happiness and joy in serving his Lord, Jesus. They don't have a desire to do many things that non-Christians freely do.

How does a person become a Christian? How can Jesus help you to get over your depression and give you purpose in your life?

You can be saved, Roger, by only ONE means, through Jesus Christ. Jesus came to Earth nearly 2,000 years ago, although previous to that He was in heaven with God the Father. Jesus is the Son of God. He began his "ministry" at age 30 and healed and preached for three years or so. He was constantly going into the wilderness to pray to follow His Father. He knew he was to die soon. A few days after he reached Jerusalem near the end of His ministry, He allowed himself to be crucified, to die for US to be SIN for US. He himself had <u>no sin at all</u>, but He loved us so much, He died for our sins.

Roger, the Bible says: "For the <u>wages</u> of sin is death..." Everyone of us has sinned. All of us, therefore, are condemned to pay the penalty - SPIRITUAL DEATH. However, those who have accepted Jesus' free gift are no longer condemned - but pardoned - they have been <u>saved</u> from Hell.

Mary Jane Warkentin

Roger,

Hi! You don't know me, but I ask you to still read this letter. I'm Scott. I live in Fresno. I heard about you approximately one year ago. This letter is about Salvation from Jesus Christ. Now you may believe that Jesus died close to two thousand years ago. I believe he rose again.

Time and time again I have begun to write to you, usually not getting more than a few line. I have already gotten an envelope and stamped and addressed it. I have not yet, at this writing, mailed anything to you.

When I heard about you, I heard that you were thinking of committing suicide. My advice to you is this: THAT YOU ACCEPT JESUS CHRIST AS YOUR PERSONAL LORD AND SAVIOUR.

You may think that Christianity is only going to church on Sundays, giving away your money and obeying rules. Only when one becomes a mature Christian do they realize that that myth is totally wrong. To the mature Christian, Christianity is great happiness and joy in serving his Lord, Jesus. They don't have a desire to do many things that non-Christian freely do.

How does a person become a Christian? How can Jesus help you to get over your depression and give you purpose in your life?

You can be saved, Roger, by only ONE means, through Jesus Christ. Jesus came to Earth nearly 2,000 years ago, although previous to that He was in heaven with God the Father. Jesus is the Son of God. He began his "Ministry" at age 30 and healed and preached for three years or so. He was constantly going into the wilderness to pray to follow His Father. He knew he was to die soon. A few days after he reached Jerusalem near the end of His ministry, He allowed himself to be crucified, to die for US, to be SIN for US. He himself had <u>he sin at all</u>, but He <u>loved</u> us so much, He died for our sins.

Lost, But Not Forever

Roger, the Bible says: "For the wages of sin is death…" Everyone of us has sinned. All of us, therefore, are condemned to pay the penalty - SPIRITUAL DEATH. However, those who have accepted Jesus' free gift are no longer condemned-but pardoned-they have been <u>saved</u> from Hell.

"Oh, God!" I burst into tears. "Scott could be a soul winner! He had never written anything like this before—at least nothing that I had ever seen. This was original, and it was good! God must have really spoken to Scott to inspire him to write such a letter.

Who was Roger anyway? I couldn't recall hearing of such a boy. I was alone in the house when I found the letter and was anxious to show it to someone. In fact, what I really wanted to do was to tell <u>everyone</u> about it! This obviously had been very hard for Scott to do, since he wasn't the outgoing type. I didn't realize our boy was that spiritually mature.

Wondering where he had heard of Roger, I decided to call Scott's Sunday School teacher and his Wednesday night youth leader. Surely one of them would have some light to throw on this mystery. But, to my bewilderment, they were as much in the dark as I. "No prayer request was ever given in our department like that," they both responded.

Regardless, it was worth sharing, and really was exciting. Everyone could pray for Roger, whoever he might be.

Yet, that wasn't the end of my amazement. Surely I must have been seeing double when, a few days later, I spotted another paper that began, "Roger." This one was under Scott's Bible on a closet shelf. It can't be bought!

Roger,
    Hi! You don't know me. I'm Scott, a 15-year old from Fresno. This letter to you is about Jesus Christ and his salvation, both of which you can have.

Mary Jane Warkentin

Approximately one year ago I heard about you. I heard that you wanted to commit suicide, Roger, accept this letter and read it through. I believe that the best, and only way to get out of your troubles of depression and meaninglessness and purposelessness is through God. Jesus tells us in the Bible (John 14:6) that "the way" is Himself-Jesus. "I am the way, the truth, and the life: no man comes unto the Father but by me," Jesus said. The real way to get out of your depression and wandering is to come to Jesus, he is <u>the only</u> way to have meaningful life here on Earth and in heaven.

Roger, Please come to Jesus. You need him because you have sinned against him and in Romans 6:23 it tells us that because you have sinned, you must die. You know you've sinned. The Bible tells us that <u>"All have sinned</u> and come short of the glory of God" (Romans 3:23) Truly, Roger, all have sinned — "There is <u>none</u> righteous, no, not one." (Romans 3:10b) God still loves us even though we've all sinned. He loved us so much Roger, that, as John 3:16 says he gave his only begotten son (Jesus), that whoever believes in (Jesus) should not perish, but have EVERLASTING LIFE")

So even though we've sinned, we can still become close to God, and be saved from our eternal death if we trust Jesus to forgive us for Jesus' gift is 100% free - it can't be bought—his GIFT IS <u>NOT</u> ON SALE. Through Jesus, you can be saved—forgiven—from all your sins you have ever done and you can have your depression ended and you can have meaning and purpose! What a gift—free—from God!

This had to be a recent letter because of its location. The other letter was in his old room, but this one was in the new bedroom. One week before his disappearance, I had moved all of Scott's belongings into a new room. This letter must have been placed in the new bedroom by Scott after the move. Therefore, it had to have been written very near the time of his disappearance. He had barely finished it in time!

Lost, But Not Forever

Obviously neither letter was in its final form. They were written on the back of printed sheets, and were not signed. Scott probably was trying to improve his first letter by adding Bible verses. The Wednesday night study of Romans had helped.

Though I did not know who Roger was, my heart already went out to him, longing for him to find the abundant life that Christ so wished to give. I stood in awe, as if in some holy Presence, as I held this second letter in my hand.

Something important ought to be done with it. But what? So when people came to visit, or someone called on the telephone, I excitedly told them all about the "Roger letters." Even the high school vice principal read one of them with interest when I dropped by to pick up Scott's unfinished art work at his school.

When his Youth for Christ director saw one, he commented, "Scott was a quiet boy. When I tried to find him at school, I not only couldn't locate him, but couldn't find anyone who knew him. I finally discovered he was hanging out in the library!"

"Yes, I know," I answered. "He liked to read books on American history at noon. Scott used to tell me all about them when he came home from school."

"Yet look at this," said the director. "What a letter he wrote! Think of the impact it can have."

It's like God multiplying the few loaves and fishes, I observed thoughtfully as he made a xerox copy of the second Roger letter to use with his young people when the opportunity arose. Who would ever think that God would use our quiet Scott in a way like this?

16

A TREACHEROUS RAFT TRIP

Shortly thereafter, we were invited to the wedding of Dave Grave's brother, which was expected to be a big affair. Since Dave was leader of search activities from our church, Joel and I were eager to be on hand to share in the festivities.

The ceremony was elegant—beautifully and tastefully done in yellow and blue, with the reception following in the social hall. We joined the line of guests to offer congratulations to the groom and his bride, and to have a taste of the wedding cake.

As we waited in the long line that extended into the yard under the glaring sun, we could hear festive voices resounding from a large crowd in the cool building...but our line didn't move! I tried to be patient and to chat with some ladies nearby, but the heat was intense, and we seemed to be going nowhere. I became irritable.

"Shall we leave?" I finally asked.

"Of course not," was my husband's reply. "You never know what very interesting person we may meet today!"

I admired his patience, but did not share his confidence. Sticking it out, however, we discovered an alternate line that made better progress and zeroed right in on the food. Soon we reached the pleasant, air-conditioned room, filled with milling guests and animated chatter. A dainty and colorful table in the center of the room looked so pretty and appetizing. The two of us filled our plates, then scanned the swarming crowd, looking for a possible place to sit down. As we wormed our way along, we leisurely stopped to converse a bit with this one and that one. Finally we reached some empty chairs, where we settled down to relax and enjoy our plates of goodies.

As we ate, Joel eyed the gentleman sitting next to him. He leaned over to me and nodded toward the man, "That's the fellow who went down the river in a raft looking for Scott," he whispered.

"It is! We've got to talk with him!" I eagerly caught a quick glance of him out of the corner of my eye. He was an adventurous-looking type in his thirties. I'd heard of this man and the precarious raft trip he and his friend had taken, but I had no idea we would ever meet either of them.

Some weeks earlier these two men had thought of looking for Scott by riding a two-man rubber raft down the river toward the lake. They had made many such rides before through other rapids. However this section of the San Joaquin River is much more dangerous than most. Dressed in rubber suits and life jackets, they launched their craft at the Kerckoff Power House by the bridge where Scott had last been seen. They had not realized the full danger of this part of the river, although Deputy Artie Cox had said the water was much too dangerous for any person to enter. One man had tried it before, and his dead body had been recovered from the lake.

Joel approached the man, who said he was the groom's brother-in-law, a married man with two daughters.

Leaning forward, I chimed in, "Are you the one who went down the San Joaquin River in a raft looking for our son, Scott Warkentin?"

"I sure am," he admitted. I swallowed hard. It was unbelievable what he had done. Not knowing whether to say thank you or to chide him for doing such a dangerous thing, I simply asked, "How was it?"

"Wild!"

"I believe it," I said. "We heard from a friend that you had this in mind, and we begged him to tell you not to go. We didn't want someone to get hurt looking for Scott, and we figured you'd get the word and call it off. Then we heard that you had made the trip anyway. Not that we didn't appreciate what you did, but we feared for you. How absolutely amazing that you lived through it!"

"It really was," he admitted. "It was a miracle of God."

"Tell us about it."

He sat back in his chair with a somber look on his face, and began, "We would never have gone if we had known how rough it would be. No one told us that you didn't want us to go. We had been on many raft trips before, and we thought we could handle it. We hoped we might locate your son's body in the water."

"But you couldn't see a thing, right?"

"We were completely disoriented. The river was treacherous, and it was impossible to stay in the raft. We kept getting thrown out, or we were sucked under by rapids and whirlpools, and it was terribly cold! When underwater, we didn't know what was up, down, or sideways. We lost one of the oars and a pair of shoes."

"It never settled down so you could stop?" I asked.

"Sometimes it was smooth. But the sides of the gorge were so steep and slick that we couldn't get hold of anything. One time we were able to get over to the side and stop. The high cliffs were so forbidding that we could not figure out a way to get up to the trail. We decided the only thing to do was to go on, so we did. One time my friend got his foot caught in the rope that went around the raft—it was almost tragic for him. At times we could not see where the river was leading, but we could hear a horrendous roar! Then, with no way to slow down or control the raft, we just plunged straight ahead over the rapids."

"I should think you'd smash against the rocks. Weren't there a lot of big boulders in there?" I inquired.

"Sure, we got plenty banged up, but the rocks didn't stop us. We just went right over them. At times we were better off not being in the raft, as it would shoot straight up after being sucked under. The strength of the current was indescribable. There was no way to fight it."

"How did you ever get out?" Joel asked.

"My friend's father had driven his pickup to the Ladd's home, which overlooks the place where the river enters the lake. He planned to wait there for his son's arrival."

Lost, But Not Forever

When the father told Mr. Ladd that the two men were coming down the river on a raft, Mr. Ladd threw up his hands in despair and said, "Oh no, that's awful! Now there will be two more bodies to fish out of the river." The father turned white when he heard the rancher's prediction, positive that his son was dead. Nevertheless, they descended the grade from the house to the river.

Finally they spotted a little speck floating on the water. It was the raft. Gradually as it loomed larger, they could make out two men in it! Reaching a part of the river near the Ladd house where the rapids loses most of its momentum, the men were able to paddle the raft with their hands over to the shore. They had made it all the way!

"My!" I gasped. "What those men on the shore must have thought when they saw you and your friend still alive!"

"The father felt just like one who had lost his son and then gotten him back alive. He was extremely grateful! Mr. Ladd helped us up the slope to his home. There we dried out and warmed up. He said that it was an absolute miracle that both of us survived!"

I remarked softly, "You wouldn't go again for anything, would you?"

"No!" he shuddered. "It was a terrifying experience! I am very glad to be alive. I just hadn't realized that it would be that dangerous."

My husband and I were thankful, too, that the fellows had come back safely. Joel was right—we did meet someone very interesting at the wedding reception that day!

Later we saw the other rafter manning a booth at the fair. We recognized his name on the placard he had placed on his table. We stopped and made ourselves known and had the privilege of talking with him also. These two men's lives touched ours in a way that expressed the caring of God's people one for another. Having children of their own, they understood our loss. Although our inner beings were horrified at what had been done, we definitely were enriched, and I especially, was glad that I had not yielded that afternoon to the irritation of a glaring sun and a long, unmoving, wedding reception line!

17

MINE SEARCHING

At Ralph's birthday party, Rick mentioned hearing of someone who had fallen into an old mine shaft in the mountains and had broken his arm in the fall. I kept thinking about that. During the initial search for Scott, one of the officials had told Joel that there were old mines from the gold rush days in the Squaw Leap area.

Finally I asked, "Joel, if someone else fell into a mine shaft, why couldn't that have happened to Scott? Maybe he's been trapped all this time and can't get out! Has anyone looked into any of the old mines up there? It even shows some of them on our map."

My husband thought it through carefully. He hadn't heard of anyone having checked the mines. Joel had assumed the search was over, but somehow we still felt uneasy about this.

"Also, that place where they were shooting rifles—has that been thoroughly searched?"

He thought it had.

My mind was obviously unsettled. "I'm concerned that Scott might have stepped on a mine shaft lid. It could have collapsed under him and he would fall into it. I can't quit thinking about all those old mines right near where Scott had been."

After some deliberation, Joel said, "I am going to see if I can get someone to go with me. I'll take off work again and we'll go check it out." I threw my arms around him in grateful approval.

On the way to Squaw Leap, Joel met two sheriffs' vehicles and flagged them down. He recognized the driver of the second, a deputy named Jerry who had participated in the first all-night search. Joel could hear the dispatcher on the car radio saying that Mr. Warkentin wanted to search the old mines. The message said that Mr. Warkentin should not be in the area alone, because of the danger. Jerry radioed that he had Mr. Warkentin with him there beside the road. The answer came back that the sheriff's department had already arranged for Joel to visit the mines, escorted by Mr. Ladd, who knew the territory well. A deputy sheriff would meet Joel at Marshall Station and accompany him to the ranch. This was where the two rafters had been picked up after their wild ride.

Joel had never expected anything like this—to be escorted around by a sheriff and a knowledgable rancher! Wasn't that something—Joel and the deputy passing each other on the road just then? Otherwise he would not have known about their well-laid plans.

"Tell him that I'll be stopping over at my daughter's place on the way up," Joel informed Jerry, and the information was radioed to the dispatcher. My husband remembered that he had phoned a cattleman to get a rough idea of where the mines were located and how best to get to them. That man must have informed the deputies who were giving him such royal treatment.

Renetta decided to go along with her dad after he told her his plans. "I'll at least go with you as far as the Marshall Station," she said. So she grabbed little Matthew just as he was, jumped into her station wagon and followed the van. They had been at Marshall Station just a few minutes when another deputy came to escort Joel to the ranch where the mines were located.

Renetta was now in a quandry. She really wanted to go farther, but she had hurriedly picked up Matthew without any food, diapers, or extra clothing. She decided to go anyway! Leaving the station wagon behind, they boarded Joel's van and followed the sheriff's car over rough dirt roads to the Ladd ranch. The ranch is nearly four hundred acres in size and it overlooks the San Joaquin River.

The Ladds came out of the house and received their visitors graciously. Mrs. Ladd immediately fell in love with little Matthew! Then, eager to be helpful, she soon busied herself fixing a nice lunch for them.

Lost, But Not Forever

"What I'd like to know," said the deputy, as he was enjoying his meal and looking out over the exquisite scenery, "is how did you come into possession of such a beautiful home site?"

"It takes diligence, perseverance...and inheritance!" Mr. Ladd explained with a grin. "My grandfather came to these parts and dug mines during the gold rush of the last century. This property has been in the family ever since." Then looking at Joel very intently, Mr. Ladd added, "You'll be interested to know that I have already checked out the old mines. I did it as soon as I heard that a boy was lost." Then he spoke more slowly and with deep emotion, "But if your heart is set on investigating the mines, then you have to do it, and I'll be glad to help."

"And I'm going to stay here and take care of Matthew," Mrs. Ladd offered, smiling.

The old rancher took Renetta and Joel out in his four-wheel-drive vehicle. The entrances to the mines they visited were all horizontal, and some had a foot or two of water in them.

"Talk softly," Mr. Ladd warned in hushed tones. "If you speak too loudly near an old mine, the sound waves could cause it to collapse."

After searching each of the four mines, Renetta and Joel were satisfied that Scott was not trapped in any one of them.

Upon returning to pick up Matthew, they were pleased to hear that he had been very good. Playing with the knobs on the old-fashioned woodburning stove was so entertaining that he never minded his wet diaper.

Before they left, Mrs. Ladd promised that she would scan the river and lake with her binoculars several times every day.

Joel saw Renetta and Matthew off for their home, and then took the van to Squaw Leap for another look. On the way he met his friend, Dave Graves, who happened to be in the vicinity. The two of them discussed possible strategies for a future search of other mines across the river.

Joel turned the van around to drive on home, but...about a mile along the way, a strong and strange fancy hit his mind—

maybe Scott is just now heading up the trail toward the parking lot! "He will come," he thought, "and no one will be there to pick him up. I must go see!" He hurried to turn the van around again, and this time he drove right into the parking lot, where there had been so much frenzied activity just a few weeks ago. Now it was inconceivably deserted. Quickly he looked around—this way and that—hoping his son had just arrived and was there waiting for him. Diligently he watched the head of the trail for Scott to appear, but to no avail—he saw no one. Joel was all alone...but God was there, so he sat and reflected on all that had happened, quietly communing with his dear heavenly Father, Whom he knew would never, never leave him nor forsake him.

Finally my husband concluded the intuition really was nothing. It was just wishful thinking; but oh, how he wished it were true! He took a last look at that trail, started the van, and guided it along the curvy road toward home, with a heavy feeling that his son had not been found. "Lord, we are just trusting You" was his conclusion for that day.

Another search of the old mines—this time on the other side of the river, was conducted the following Saturday. Joel, Dave Graves, and Rick crossed the river bridge and hiked downstream.

"Did you know that a guy looking for Scott stepped on a rattlesnake the other day?"

"He did! Did it bite him?" Rick wondered, grimacing.

"It never touched him. He jumbled off pretty fast, and I guess he and the rattler each went about their business. There'll be a lot more of those snakes in here now that it's beginning to warm up."

The three men trudged along, thoroughly screening likely areas between the river and the ridge, but they could not find a single evidence of a mine entrance.

"They've probably all collapsed after this long a time," Rick remarked. "It's been about a hundred years since anyone has been mining gold in these parts." Also, these mines had not been carefully protected like those on Mr. Ladd's property.

Lost, But Not Forever

"Here we are," observed Joel, "with all these detailed maps—mines marked right on them—and with directions from knowledgeable old-timers. If we can't even find the mine entrances, then how could Scott ever have gotten into one?"

"No, I just don't think he could," answered Rick.

The three searchers were all utterly fatigued. Their muscles ached and their feet were sore. Joel sank down wearily on a pile of rocks; Rick slumped onto the grass. After a few minutes Dave sat too, and he remarked thoughtfully, "Scott is probably looking down from wherever he is, and saying, 'What are you guys making all this hassle over me for? I'm in good hands.'"

They gave up looking for the mine openings.

"It's really no great surprise to me," Joel reflected. "I figure Scott probably fell into the river. But if you have an idea of somewhere else he might be, you must take that million-to-one chance. You go and look, just in case."

"You're right," commented Dave. "You can't think the rest of your life, 'Oh, if only I had followed my intuition! He might have been there!'"

18

NEVER ALONE

While Joel and the others were looking for abandoned mines, I realized that I'd better do some grocery shopping. With the ladies of the church no longer bringing food to our home, I needed to resume my usual duties in the kitchen. I was sure that I'd completely forgotten how to cook! And even if I hadn't, probably no one would want to eat my dinners after the sumptuous fare we'd been having. Nevertheless, I made preparations, hopped into the car, and was on my way.

"Be careful for nothing" (Philippians 4:6). I hadn't been traveling far before this Bible verse began making its way into my mind. I knew these words meant "be anxious for nothing" or "don't be anxious about anything."

"How can I not be anxious?" I mumbled, arguing with the Bible as I drove along. "My son whom I love so much—my Scottie—is lost in the mountains, or drowned in a river. I don't know where he is, or what has happened to him, and I'm not supposed to be anxious about it? I AM anxious!"

"Be anxious for nothing." The words came softly again, so gently.

"I CAN'T," I retorted out loud, as the usual stream of travelers buzzed by, unaware of the struggle in my heart.

"But by prayer and supplication..."

"I've prayed and prayed!" I responded almost in anger.

"Let your requests be made known to God."

"I've done that, too," I said.

"And the peace of God, which passeth all understanding shall keep your hearts and minds through Christ Jesus" (Philippians 4:7).

"Oh, give me that peace!" I earnestly pled.

Nothing but silence.

Lost, But Not Forever

Softly I began to say the words over to myself, yet audibly, "Be anxious for nothing...be anxious for nothing...be anxious for nothing...be anxious for nothing..." As I repeated it again and again and again, in a quiet voice, the peace that I needed so badly began to come. Slowly and steadily my anxiety was metamorphosized. In its place a serenity emerged, a mental calmness, a composure, even contentment, as I felt the presence of a divine force that seemed to flood the car with pure love! Truly that was "the peace which passeth understanding."

The phone was ringing as I carried my groceries into the house. "This is Channel 47 calling. We heard that your husband has gone up to Squaw Leap to investigate old mines." This television station had been much interested in our case, and had kept the public well informed with stories and pictures. I wondered what they wanted now. "Does this mean the search for your son is not over yet?" the man asked.

"Yes, I believe that's so."

"Then we would like to come to your house and interview you for this evening's newscast. We'll be there in forty-five minutes." He hung up before I could answer.

"Forty-five minutes? Me? Again? On T.V.?" I said it all to myself as I put the phone into its place. If it weren't in such a context, I'd really relish this. "Well," I mumbled, "why not try to enjoy it anyway?"

I checked my hair first; the other time it had looked too flat—way too flat on top. There wouldn't be time to set it. I'd have to make something of what was there, so I fluffed it up as best I could. I didn't dare work at it too long, but it was important. There, that would have to do.

Then I quickly scanned the living room. The last time I had arranged it all so carefully, even moved furniture around, thinking, "Will they use this corner? How's that background?" Every spot had to be perfect. But the cameraman had shot the whole thing outdoors in the front yard. They didn't even come into the house! I wasn't going to fall for that one again. I let the living room go.

"What will I say?" The thought jerked me into reality. That was the important part. Quickly I tried to collect my thoughts, and I was soon practicing a speech in front of the large gilt-framed mirror on the wall, while glancing at my watch every few minutes.

"We'd all assumed that our son, Scott, drowned in the river," I rehearsed. "But I got to thinking about other possibilities—like all the shooting that took place nearby. Also, there are old mine shafts that he could have fallen into. My husband has gone up particularly to investigate the mines. The search is not over, and we still have hope that our boy may be found. God has been with us all the time, and has helped us to cope with every difficult situation."

"There, how did that sound?" I asked myself approvingly. I worked on memorizing every word, in case I became flustered. I barely had time to call a few friends on the telephone.

"I'm going to be on T.V. Would you like to listen?"

Then it began to rain, just a little. Maybe the television crew would call it all off!

But they didn't. There they were at my door!

I greeted the two men, and stepped out into the drizzle to pose for the cameras.

"We can't take pictures in the rain," the photographer advised me. "We will use your living room." So I invited him in, and as the camera rolled, I recited my little prepared speech. I suppose the room was clean enough and the backgrounds were appropriate; I really didn't bother to look. One thing I was sure of—I never could outguess a cameraman.

Sleep eluded me that night. As I lay there wide awake—listening to my husband's unrhythmical breathing—I tried to put myself into God's place. "I've been doing so much talking, dear Lord," I mused. "You did meet me in such a special way in the car this afternoon. Your love was so glorious! But most of the time, I haven't given You a chance to get a word in edgewise." It

Lost, But Not Forever

was true—my prayers had been so constant, like a beggar's never-ending plea. I needed to stop more, and listen.

"Maybe You have a message to say to me now, Lord."

I told Him, "I'll be quiet in my thinking and give You a chance, just in case." Then, realizing that an empty mind can be a demon's opportunity, I added, "But let me be sure that it is You, Lord, if I do hear something."

I tried to go blank, which wasn't easy with my active mind. I cast aside any thought of my own which tried to intrude. All was quiet for about one full minute. Then these words, which were clearly from an outside source, very slowly entered my mind: DON'T WORRY. IT'S ALL IN MY HANDS.

"Thank you," was all I could murmur, and I knew He was there.

"I'm going to put Scott's picture in the newspaper," I announced to everyone the next day. "Why haven't we done that before?" We all realized that everyone had been too busy to think of it.

"You'll have to produce a black-and-white portrait of your son," I was told at the newspaper office. "This colored one won't print up well."

What was I to do? I had already gone through my pictures of Scott thoroughly, and was happy to have found this colored one! Scott was the last of five children and we had not taken as many pictures of him as of the others, especially good, recent ones. They were all in color.

"Try the high school yearbook," the reporter suggested. "His picture should be in there."

When I called the high school, I was informed that the book was not out yet, but the secretary offered to do what she could to help. She contacted the yearbook advisor, who volunteered to have her student staff check through all the pictures they had taken that year to see if Scott was in any of them. It would be done that very afternoon.

"The picture is in the office waiting for you!" I was told when I inquired the next morning. The school had taken a little one-inch-square color photo from Scott's student card, had it photographed in black and white, and blown up to three-by-five. It was perfect!

In the next day's newspaper, the following caption appeared under Scott's picture:

MISSING

Scott Warkentin, 15, a son of Joel and Mary Jane Warkentin has been missing since April 2. He was last seen above Millerton Lake in the Squaw Leap area. He is a 6-footer and very thin. He was wearing a brown corduroy jacket, tan shirt, and black tennis shoes. He has long blond hair. Anyone with information as to his whereabouts is asked to call the Fresno or Madera County Sheriff's Department.

19

A TIME OF ANXIETY

One thing was left that I felt must be done, and that was to put out an all-points bulletin on Scott, in case he somehow had wandered off or had been kidnapped. Police authorities would be notified all over the state, and even in some surrounding states.

After this, the rigorous search would definitely be considered over. If nothing turned up, the Warkentins would collect themselves and go on. After all, there were four children left. We still had three boys—wasn't that enough? Yet, like the shepherd looking for the one lost sheep out of a hundred, our thoughts those days were almost exclusively on the one lost child.

I phoned the sheriff's office and was told that I could call back Monday, when the deputies would be in their offices, though the deputies who had been working on Scott's case would be away then also—at a convention on "Expert Searching".

"Good," I thought, "a convention on expert searching! Maybe they will learn something new about searching. Scott's case will probably be discussed." I was given the name of a lieutenant whom I could contact on Monday.

Rather than wait for the convention to finish, I called first thing Monday morning. "I'll have to look into the records to find out what already has been done," he informed me. "Call tomorrow, and I'll have it ready. Check with me after four o'clock."

"Tomorrow" sounded like such a long time, especially after having already waited over the weekend. If Scott were alive somewhere, he might be just barely existing and one day could mean the difference. And four o'clock is so late in the day. "God, if he is living, please keep him alive until all this goes through and they can find him. What am I going to do, pray for

Scott all the rest of my life when he probably is dead and already safe in heaven? I guess I'll have to."

Tuesday afternoon finally did come. At four o'clock sharp I made my phone call to the sheriff's department, and I reached the lieutenant immediately. He told me that be would call me back for sure the next morning.

"The next morning? Not until Wednesday! What a letdown! This goes on and on. I can't get that guy to do anything!" I brewed. Up to that point I had been treated like a celebrity when I asked anyone for help. Once when I had called for Artie Cox, the secretary ran out to the parking lot to catch him as he was leaving for home. Artie came all the way back into the building to talk with Scott's mom. That was the way it had been. Now I couldn't even get anyone to put Scott's name and description on an all-points bulletin! It seemed like a simple enough thing to do.

"Everyone thinks I'm crazy to consider that Scott might be alive," I told myself. "But he could be! If he wandered out of the area, he may be merely walking around, hoping to see something familiar." I could picture him sauntering aimlessly along, living on plants and stream water. Perhaps he was even healthier now than ever before on such a diet.

As I thought it over, I wondered if Scott did see a deserted cabin full of food, would his moral principals keep him from breaking in because it did not belong to him? Also, he had a unique shyness about him; he might not admit to a stranger that he was lost, so they would not help him. He felt perfectly at ease and talkative with his family, but—as far as I know—he had never initiated conversation with someone he didn't know. Some of these things bothered me now. Would Scott miss an opportunity to be rescued just because of bashfulness? I wasn't sure what he might do; and yet, he might surprise us! "He's probably expecting to spend the rest of his life this way—all by himself— if he's not half-dead by now." As hard as I tried, I could not continue to accept Walter's conclusion that he had drowned and there was no other possibility.

Lost, But Not Forever

Sometimes I wondered if he might eat some poisonous plants up there in the mountains. But my grocer assured me, "No, be wouldn't do that; they all taste terribly bitter if they are poisonous."

"How do you know that?"

"Oh, I tasted them when I was a kid."

Even that was a consolation.

Since it had been almost a month since Scott disappeared, my mental image of him kept oscillating between that of a healthy young man walking around because he didn't know how to get back home, and my precious son lying in agony somewhere in a half-coma, gasping his final breaths.

By Wednesday when the person from the sheriff's office was to call, I was emotionally exhausted. I was tired of answering phone calls—except, of course, from that elusive lieutenant. I wanted to go outside and pull weeds! It was plain to see that there were plenty of those intruding plants in my yard. "I just might enjoy pulling their heads off," I said. "But I might not hear the telephone when it rings; that officer is supposed to call today." However, I just couldn't make myself stay in the house any longer. I needed something a bit refreshing. So I opened all the back doors and windows wide, placed the phone as close as possible to the door, and went out into the big back yard.

How good it was to be in the fresh out-of-doors! The trees were as tall and stately as ever, and a few fleecy clouds drifted lazily in the blue-gray sky. Fragrant long-neglected roses were in full bloom, and the May sun felt warm on my back. It was still God's big, wide, wonderful world. Everything around me was the same—only I had changed. I had lost a son, and it was heart-rending.

The ground was moist and the weeds pulled easily. Flowers and bushes seemed to be looking more comfortable already. It felt kind of good to be getting dirty.

Oh...there...the telephone was ringing. I really almost forgot. Jumping up, I rushed inside, hobbling a little from being down on my haunches. I quickly refreshed what I was going to

Mary Jane Warkentin

say...but it was a friend wondering how I was. At least now I knew that I would hear the telephone from the yard when the man called to put Scott on an all-points bulletin. It should be soon now.

The day lingered on, and I was becoming impatient.

"He said he would call; why hasn't he done what he said he would do?" I was becoming angrier. "I'll give that officer one more half hour, and then I'm going to call him...no, I won't wait one more minute for him; I am going to call that man right now!"

Storming into the house, I headed for the phone. I had easily memorized the sheriff department's number by this time, so I dialed it quickly.

"May I speak to the lieutenant, please?"

"I'm sorry. He has left for home."

I couldn't believe my ears! Rage rushed up into my face. I wanted to blow up at the person on the other end of the line. It was only three o'clock in the afternoon, and he had already gone home—forgetting all about me! I was furious.

Trying terribly hard to control myself, I said as softly as I could, "This is Mary Jane Warkentin, the mother of Scott Warkentin, who is lost in the mountains. I wanted to put Scott's name on an all-points bulletin. Is there anyone there who can do this for me? He's been gone three and a half weeks, and he could be lying somewhere half dead. This really should be done right now."

The voice interrupted, "Yes, that's true. I'll have him call you first thing in the morning." She hung up.

"What in the world is the matter with that guy? This is not some little social call; it's very important business. It's life and death. First thing in the morning!" I yelled frantically, "I waited all weekend until Monday; then they said to wait till Tuesday; for sure it would be done on Wednesday; and now he puts me off until Thursday! What's so hard about doing that little thing? I can't wait any longer! I can't stand it!...I can't...I can't...I CAN'T!"

Lost, But Not Forever

I screamed and cried vehemently. It wasn't for me; it was for Scott. Heaving sobs turned into wails. No one was around so I just cut loose—unable to control myself. I was absolutely crushed.

"I can't cope—I don't know how to cope! What'll I do?...Oh God! Please help me!" Tears poured down endlessly while I paced the floor and sobbed loudly. I just couldn't quit. It was too much. The pressure was too heavy. "Doesn't he have any heart for a boy who may be dying right now?" I screamed. "Doesn't he care about me? I'm nobody to him. Nobody cares about me—or my son. God may care, but He just leaves me to suffer like this!"

For the first and only time in my life I understood how a person could want to commit suicide. "That's why they reach for drugs or a bottle," I thought. "If you can't cope, you can't cope." I just didn't know how to grapple with this thing.

Besides, I was lonely—depressingly lonely. I had always thought that lonesome people should call up their forlorn friends to console one another. But that's not what I wanted. If no one was going to help me with Scott, I didn't need anybody else. I just wanted my family—<u>all</u> of my family!

The door opened. Joel was home from teaching school. I tried to suddenly compose myself, but it didn't work—out it poured—floods of tears...the whole works! He put his consoling arms about me, but I couldn't turn it off, even for him.

Somehow I managed to put a semblance of supper on the table, and the sobs did subside somewhat while we ate.

Then the phone rang; it was a close friend.

"Hi, Babe." That was her pet name for me. "Are you listening to channel 53?"

"No."

"Then turn it on. That man who died and came back to life is talking right now."

The man on television, Marvin Ford, was speaking about heaven. He had suffered a heart attack at work a few years before, and while in the hospital experienced death and life

Mary Jane Warkentin

waging warfare within him. He felt his spirit leave, and soon he began to see an iridescent light beckoning him into the most beautiful city he had ever seen.

I thought of Scott as I listened. Had my son traveled to that city? I was spellbound to find out what the man saw there.

Mr. Ford said that it was immense, splendid, and overwhelmingly bright. He saw the throne of God and one resplendent light emanating from the right of it. He recognized the light as Jesus, his Savior. Jesus welcomed the man into His presence, and he began to worship Christ.

All this was like healing salve to me as I listened. I reveled in the thought of a sparkling city more exquisite than earthlings can imagine—a place where Jesus is! Its description in the Bible came to my mind as I imagined Scott there in the midst of it all:

> The building of the wall of it was of jasper: and the city was pure gold, like unto clear glass. And the foundations of the wall of the city were garnished with all manner of precious stones...And the twelve gates were twelve pearls: every several gate was one pearl: and the street of the city was pure gold, as it were transparent glass (Revelation 21:18,19,21).

> And he shewed me a pure river of water of life, clear as crystal, proceeding out of the throne of God and and of the Lamb...And they shall see his face; and his name shall be in their foreheads (Revelation 22: 1, 4).

> And God shall wipe away all tears from their eyes; and there shall be no more death, neither sorrow, nor crying, neither shall there be any more pain: for the former things are passed away (Revelation 21:4).

Despite these comforting thoughts, sleep eluded me that night. My spirits had been greatly relieved and lifted from thinking about heaven, but now it all came back and I had to run for the tissue box again.

Lost, But Not Forever

"Do you want me to be quiet, or to say something?" Joel asked awkwardly, trying to help, as I crawled into bed.

"It doesn't make any difference," I moaned, unable to hold back my emotion. "I'll go into the other room so you can get some sleep. You can't have any peace with me bawling."

"No, you stay right here," he insisted, as he held me close.

I sobbed uncontrollably on into the night.

Finally, I thought of something that made me stop crying. "There are only three possible alternatives," I said to myself: "(1) Scott is dead (2) God doesn't want Scott to be found. (3) God wants Scott to be found, but not yet. If the first were true, Scott was in heaven. After all his terrible suffering, and ours, if I really had to, I could find a way to live with that. If God didn't want Scott to be found, then should I want it? Didn't I always tell myself that I had no desire for anything that was against God's wishes? And if the last alternative were true, Scott would be found. I could wait for that. In these thoughts I found comfort. It seemed that every time I fell just so low emotionally, God had something to lift me up!

Oh, who are we to judge another when we ourselves are ignorant of their circumstances? "Judge not, that ye be not judged," the Bible says (Matthew 7:1). If I had known why the lieutenant had not called back about the all-points bulletin, I would have been more tolerant of his actions. I called him myself the next morning. I was asked to come to his office. He told me that his brother had died, and for that reason he had been unable to return my calls. I had become so wrapped up in my own problems that I had forgotten that others might be hurting also. Death—it intrudes its head uninvited, regardless of time or convenience. With this I could sympathize, and I forgave him.

Now, at last the final simple task that was my last hope of finding my boy alive was performed. All sheriffs' departments in California and other nearby regions were alerted to the circumstances of Scott Warkentin's disappearance. It was a great relief to know that this was done.

Mary Jane Warkentin

No one could ever say that a stone had been left unturned. Our family could face the future with confidence that every possible effort had been made to recover our loved one.

Since there was no plot in a cemetery containing the remains of our son, Joel and I wanted some type of memorial in remembrance of Scott. We were especially interested in the Evangel Home—the haven for homeless women and children. This institution was just launching a new extension ministry: a halfway house.

Merabelle, the superintendent of Evangel Home, had invited Joel and me to have Sunday dinner there. It was the only time she had personally invited us to a meal; she did not know that we had anything special concerning the home on our hearts. After the dinner, Joel discussed with her the idea of establishing a fund to help buy a building for the Evangel Home's extension ministry. This fund would be a memorial to Scott.

Merabelle thought this was a fine idea, and it was agreed that Joel would present it at the monthly board meeting, which happened to be the following evening. Joel made his presentation, and the group officially established the Scott Warkentin Memorial Fund. Joel had felt for some time the urge to make a large contribution to a special project of the Lord's work, and this provided the opportunity. Thus the program was underway. Many took advantage of this, and $1850 has been raised for the project. One couple enclosed this note:

> We, as a family, are enclosing a memorial in Scott Warkentin's name, because we know how near to the hearts of the Warkentins Evangel Home and the work you do in Christ's name is. And we know how important Jesus was to Scott here on earth. We appreciated the way he shared his faith in the high school Sunday class where we have been sharing our time and our commitment this year.
>
> Love in Christ,
Abe and Becky

20

AN UNUSUAL BOAT RIDE

After Scott had been missing almost six weeks, we concluded that he must have fallen into the river and was lodged under a rock somewhere on the bottom, and that his body would never be recovered. There was no place else to look or inquire.

Joel had taken out two life insurance policies for Scott. But the insurance companies would not pay off unless a death certificate could be produced. One company obligingly said it would pay after seven years.

So, Joel went to the county clerk's office to see about getting a death certificate, since all the authorities had concluded that Scott was in the river. Certainly that seemed to be the only logical explanation of what had happened to him. The gentleman at the county clerk's office was very courteous, but he said such a document could not be issued without a body. The only other possibility was to present a certificate establishing the fact of death and a sheriff's report at a court hearing. If the judge felt the evidence warranted it, he would sign the document and a death certificate would be issued. Joel planned to go the following Monday to start such proceedings.

The next afternoon, Saturday, Joel was in the drive-way working on his van when a car came driving up slowly and stopped in front of the house. A gentleman got out and asked, "Are you Mr. Warkentin?"

"Yes, I am."

The man pulled an official identification card from his pocket to show Joel. He was a deputy coroner!

"We think we have found your son, Scott," he said.

Joel listened intently as the man explained that a body fitting Scott's decription had been accidently found in the water at the head of Millerton Lake. Because of the condition of the body, positive identification had not been made. Scott's dentist would have to supply the final proof.

Joel invited the coroner inside and began looking for me.

"Are you calling, Joel?" I answered from the garage where I was working on the laundry.

He came to where I was. "Yes," he answered soberly. "There is a man here I'm sure you will want to meet."

"I'll be right in."

A timid sort of fear struck me as I wondered what was going on. The man was standing in the living room when I entered.

"Mary Jane," Joel said, "This is the deputy coroner of Fresno County.

I was suddenly paralyzed—it went all through me! "This must be it!" I thought.

Joel looked at me and said, "This man thinks they have found Scott's body." It shouldn't have been a shock, and yet I was stunned. It was like a big chunk of me was being torn away, never to be replaced. I wondered if I would begin to cry, but I didn't.

"I will call our dentist," Joel told the coroner. He was being so brave.

The dentist was not at home, but his wife promised to contact him and have him call the coroner's office at once.

"I will take care of it from here and call you back as soon as the dentist has made positive identification," the coroner said kindly.

"If it is Scott, when can we see him?" Joel asked.

"I think it would be best for you not to view the body," the coroner replied. "Remember him as you last saw him. His body is now at the morgue."

"Can't they identify him by his clothes?" I said, feeling a deeper numbness setting in.

The man said that all of the clothing had been washed off and the hair was gone. I was shocked. What was left was not recognizable as Scott. An autopsy had been performed and there was no evidence of foul play. The coroner left his card, promising to call as soon as he knew anything.

"If that dentist goes to Scott and checks his teeth, I think that will be the greatest act of love anyone has done yet," I proclaimed, "and I'm going to tell him so when I see him."

Before long the coroner phoned to tell us that the body was Scott's! Our dentist talked with Joel and confirmed what the coroner had told us. The fillings in his teeth checked out to be exactly like those on Scott's dental X-rays.

Scott's body had been found at last and this time it was real! The search was over. Joel and I were sad, but relieved.

Now we could go to sleep at night and know where Scott was. At long last we knew what happened to our boy. It was much as suspected, but, of course, the exact circumstances of Scott's death will always be unknown to us. Only God has that knowledge.

We tend to believe that the accident happened very soon after Scott left us on the first day—that he never was "lost." As he left Joel at the bridge, he probably headed right for that big beautiful waterfall, then walked alongside the river a bit, got too close, perhaps stepping on an insecure rock, and—after a few awfully fearful seconds of plunging a hundred feet or so down the bank— was soon tenderly ushered into the presence of his loving Heavenly Father.

I thought of the many hours I had spent by the pool waiting during Red Cross swimming lessons to be sure of Scott's safety—that he would be "drown-proof." But there was no chance for the best swimmer in that icy, churning pit!

A feeling of jealousy came over me because God had him, when I wanted to raise him myself instead. But I remembered my mother's words, "Our children are loaned to us by God for a few years."

But I recalled the blessings as well.

It was amazing to realize that all during Scott's absence, his bed was not in the Warkentin house. About two weeks before the accident, Wayne's apartment mate had needed a bed in his new room, so Joel offered him Scott's bed temporarily. Wayne and Ralph had just moved out of the house, so there were other places where Scott could sleep. I thought at the time, "This is certainly strange, taking Scott's bed away from him," but it seemed the most sensible thing to do; the two spare beds that the other boys had left were a matched set that we did not want to separate. What a blessing it turned out to be for us during those six weeks that we did not have to look at the empty bed in which Scott had slept! God in His kindness relieved us of this emotional trauma.

Later, we phoned the man in Los Banos who had found Scott's body. Both Joel and I talked with him. We were glad to be able to thank him personally.

He told us about discovering the body. He, his wife, and their thirteen-year-old twin sons had been camping at Millerton Lake for the weekend. They were in a motor boat on the lake and decided to go up the San Joaquin River looking for driftwood. They were curious to see how far up the river a boat could go. As they were cruising along, the current was becoming quite swift. Suddenly an object appeared on the water; it must have just surfaced.

They were not sure what it was. As they maneuvered the boat closer, they saw that it was a human body. They had read in the paper of our son's disappearance and immediately thought it might be he. Two fishermen agreed to stay there with the body while the man and his family went to report the finding.

"After leaving our boys with friends on shore," the boater went on, "we directed the state rangers to the approximate area. But when we all arrived, we could not find the body, or the fishermen. We started downstream, leaving the rangers to mark the area. About a quarter of a mile down river, we again spotted the body. We hailed the rangers, and I assisted in recovering it."

Scott's remains were thus picked up about five miles from the bridge where he had last been seen by his father six weeks previously.

Renetta's foster girls happened to be picnicking at the lake at that very time. They saw nothing of the discovery being made so close at hand.

The weather had turned hot the day before, hovering around the hundred-degree mark. This had hastened the snow melt in the mountains and caused the flow of the river to almost double. This well could have dislodged Scott's body from a rock against which it was caught.

His body was spotted in the same vicinity where the neighbor had been boating the day he saw a vulture go down. The two occasions were two weeks apart. "Now I can go fishing again," he said. "I never felt like fishing any more when I should be looking for Scott." No doubt many searchers had passed by the place where Scott was under the water, but they had been unable to see him. Now Joel would have no need to struggle with the courts for possession of a death certificate.

21

A DOUBLE PORTION

"Festo!" I remembered with a start. I had almost forgotten. "We're supposed to be counselors at the Festo meeting tonight." Festo Kivengere, bishop of a church in Uganda, Africa, was in the United States having evangelistic meetings and was to be in Fresno for just one evening.

"We won't be going tonight," Joel announced to me, "since Scott's body has just been found today."

I started thinking that over a little. My thoughts went back over the entire six week period of Scott's absence. All through this time I had continued to teach my weekly ladies' Bible class and two other Bible studies each month. True, Scott had been the subject of much of it, because I tried to share what God was doing in my life. Somehow, when the time came to speak to a group, the Lord always made me strong enough to do it, and I was myself lifted spiritually by the experience. The first time (at Evangel Home) I had wondered about it, but I soon came to depend upon God's enabling power so I could be a blessing to others. He always came through! And I was richer for it. To me, this is a miracle. I never broke down when I was presenting a lesson or telling my story. When I cried—which happened every day—it was when it didn't matter. Also, Joel and I had continued going to Sunday School and church—morning and evening—although twice I had found it necessary to leave for home because of tears that wouldn't quit, but that was all right.

There were times when a person would say something that touched a soft spot, and I would begin to cry. I think everyone should accept that as being okay. I didn't want a person to leave me if I cried. I liked it better if he stayed, treated me gently, and let me know that he was there, and that I was doing only what would be expected of someone in my position. But usually in a church service it was just a matter of a few tears rolling down

Lost, But Not Forever

during one of the songs. They were easily wiped away. Keeping active in God's service had definitely been a therapy for both of us. I didn't want to stop now. I felt as if my testimony might be more meaningful than when things were rosy.

I had often thought that God spared me from having heavy burdens of my own, so I could be stronger to help lift others. I assumed that I would be much too weak to bear anything heavy myself. The Lord surely knew this, and would continue to relieve me of great personal difficulties so I could be free to serve Him. But now I better understood the words, "My grace is sufficient for thee: for my strength is made perfect in weakness. Most gladly therefore will I rather glory in my infirmities, that the power of Christ may rest upon me. Therefore I take pleasure in infirmities, in reproaches, in necessities, in persecutions, in distresses for Christ's sake: for when I am weak, then am I strong" (2 Corinthians 12: 9-19).

I am not a strong person. I have physical, emotional, and nervous limitations within which I must live. These are often bothersome to me and cramp my style; I am not able to do many things I would like to do, and I have to take a lot of unwanted rest. I am weak, but it is better that way, because then God's almighty power is more evident in my life. I found out that I can lift others better when I have had burdens of my own.

So, in spite of the circumstances, or perhaps because of them, I felt that I should go to the Festo meeting that night. I might even get to lead someone to Christ!

"I really want to go," I said. And Joel decided to go with me.

The music at the meeting was very slow, majestic, and exultant. The words spoke of the grandeur and soveignty of Almighty God—His love, power, and wisdom. It was just what we needed—nourishment to our souls. Festo gave a powerful sermon, and then came the invitation.

A few came to the front, but it looked as though there was an excess of counselors. I was so anxious to be of help to someone! Yet, not wanting to put myself forward and take that joy away from someone else (even though I had gone through the counselor training) I consoled myself with the thought that I was not needed by anyone that night.

Just then I spotted a child in the group of folks who had come forward in answer to the invitation. There was no one with a counselor's badge nearby. I looked around again to be sure and then down at my own badge, but only the girl's mother stood with her. So I approached the woman saying, "I am one of the counselors; I would like to speak with the girl, if I may."

"Oh, yes, of course," answered her mom. "We came forward as a family." Glancing about I noticed the father was there too. I found myself with more than I had expected!

"Fine. Then let's all go sit down over here and we can talk," I suggested.

Thankfully, Joel had his eye on the situation too, and he soon began conversing with the man, and the two of them went off together.

I was then privileged to talk and pray with this mother and her daughter, who both wanted to come back to the Lord and have a closer walk with Him. I was able to share, not only my faith in God's love with them, but also the strength, peace, and hope only He can give in our darkest hours.

So I was given a double portion! In spite of a sad day, my heart was happy.

22

TO GOD BE THE GLORY

At church the next morning it was announced: "Probably you have heard the news by now that the body of Scott Warkentin was found yesterday in the river. In a way, it's a great relief to the Warkentin family to know what has happened to Scott. They need our prayers; so before we do anything else, let's join together, as one of our members leads us."

The prayer leader[2] was a high school athletic coach with a robust singing voice, which he uses constantly in the Lord's service. He is loved by all. Slowly, he walked to the platform.

"Our heavenly Father," he prayed, "it is the power of a risen Christ that we lean upon today. This morning, as we think of Scott and the life he lived upon this earth, we thank You for letting us know him and have the joy of being with him. We thank You for the faith he expressed in You, Lord. We are grateful that Scott is with You this morning. We are glad he has entered his eternal day, and that he is there rejoicing.

"We thank You for conquering death for us, and for the Scripture that says, 'I am the resurrection and the life: he that believeth in me, though he were dead, yet shall he live: and whosoever liveth and believeth in me shall never die.' Amen."

Then, before the regular message of the morning, a devout and faithful member of the church felt impelled to speak. With great emotion he said, "This morning I am thinking about Scott. Scott was in my Sunday School class. I was his leader, yet he had impressed me with how little I know about the Bible. His life has convicted me. Revelation 3:15 talks about whether you are hot or cold; if you're lukewarm, God is going to spew you out of His mouth. This bothers me.

---

[2] Jack Hannah

"Last weekend we were at a couples' conference. I heard a fellow tell about how the water runs faster in the middle of the river. But the funny thing is that, as you get to the sides of the river, it slows down; there are places on the sides where the water even turns around and will be going upstream! This really hit me this morning. Scott's life was very close to God, and he knew a lot about the Bible. He was in the middle of the river. He was involved!"

Tears welled up in this teacher's eyes as he continued, "I thought about my life, and how many times I'd gone down the river of life, when suddenly I had found myself over to the side, and I'd been going backwards! How many of us are in an idle pool that is kind of circling?

"Up on the search, as we were having lunch, we were looking across the river and watching a piece of wood. That river was going like sixty; it was flowing so fast, with tons of water rushing down. But there was a place over there where a piece of wood was just going around in circles, even though it was close to the real action, but it was doing nothing. Get in the game! I would encourage you to get involved—to get your life right with God. We never know! Look at Scott, another example this morning.

"As I was doing a lot of thinking about this, some words came to my mind. I was trying to think of words that all started with the same letter. I thought of 'Christ,' of 'church,' 'convicted,' 'confessed,' 'committed,' 'confident.'" He began to choke with tears, "'challenged'. it's terrible to be emotional, but I can't help it.

"Then I thought of other words that express how I am many, many times. I'm 'comfortable' where I am. It's 'convenient.' If my religion is convenient, then I'm 'complacent.' I wish we could get those three words—'comfortable,' 'convenient,' and 'complacent'—out of our Christian lives!"

He pulled a white handkerchief out of his back pocket and wiped the pulpit where his tears had fallen. "Sorry I got it wet," he said, as he headed back to his seat. But the congregation

Lost, But Not Forever

wasn't sorry about the tears, for they had been touched by the presence ot God's Spirit that day.

We made arrangements for a private burial. Monday afternoon the family gathered, along with a few friends, in front of a casket containing the long-sought body of Scott Warkentin.

As soon as I stepped out of the car at the cemetery, I saw the gray coffin across the way. I couldn't imagine how I was going to go over there by it. A deluge of tears broke forth!

"What am I going to do, Wayne?" I asked seriously of my oldest son, who had already headed in the direction of the gravesite. He came back to me. I gazed up into his face, lamenting, "I'm going to bawl my eyes out through this whole thing! I can't go over there!" What I used to know as Scott was in that box, and I loved every bit that was left of him. I knew his spirit was in heaven, but some of him was over there in that casket too. How we all had looked for that body! We'd put our heart and soul into it. Oh, so many people had, at great sacrifice to themselves and to those around them.

Wayne put his arm around me. He was six feet four inches tall, but I looked down at the ground as he said fondly, "Aw, Mom, it's okay. You don't have to try not to cry." I felt so relieved that I hugged my son warmly in appreciation.

And what do you suppose happened? I stopped crying. Suddenly I felt strong. I was able to go over there, and even talk to the people. And I had joy—I really did!

The minister read Psalm 21 and made a few comments.

A floral arrangement from the family decorated the casket.

After a short service, Joel handed me the floral spray to take home if I wished. My close friend (the one that calls me "Babe") walked over, gave me a hug, and told me that the yellow flowers in the bouquet I held were for the streets of gold where Scott was walking; the white flowers designated the perfection he now enjoyed; and the blue ones meant that he was far above the sky in a land that is fairer than day. I added, "And the green is for

Mary Jane Warkentin

new growth. This experience is going to help me grow stronger in the Lord I love." We exchanged smiles.

She said, "The green is also for new life—the many souls who will come to know Jesus because of this tragedy!" We both were encouraged by that thought.

When we arrived home, Joel stopped at the box to pick up our mail. Among bills and solicitations he found a letter from our niece in Illinois. We knew that she and her husband would be having a baby soon, and that is what it was: an announcement of a new little life in the family, along with the baby's picture.

"What an adorable baby!" I gasped. How touching—the moment we arrived home from burying our son, we received news of a precious new boy born into the family! It couldn't have been more perfectly timed. All I could add were the words from a familiar Bible verse, which was now fresh with new meaning: "The Lord gave, and the Lord hath taken away; blessed be the name of the Lord" (Job 1:21).

Joel, Mary Jane, and son, Ralph, arrived home from the cemetary to hear of a new baby born into their family.

Lost, But Not Forever

Now a memorial service was in order. It would be held on Thursday night so more people could attend. We wanted it to be a time of victory and triumph—honoring Scott's entrance into heaven, and bringing glory to God.

My ninety-two-year-old father and his wife of twelve years, Ruth, wanted to come to the service from their home in Northern California, but felt they were too old to travel. They ventured out anyway, and made the all-day bus trip by themselves, arriving just in time to join the family for the church service. It meant so very much to us to have them with us—especially to me.

Our family arrived in time to greet the congregation as they entered. Joel, the children, and I circulated among the crowd receiving embraces and condolences from new friends and old. We were surprised and very pleased to see so many unexpected people. It was with a sense of awe that we stood in the foyer surrounded by such sincere love and concern.

The church was packed. Seats were put up in the foyer. All the family was seated toward the front—I between my husband and my father.

The minister's wife—in her usual inspiring manner—played a medley of familiar hymns, followed by the reading of Scripture verses about heaven. The athletic coach sang "Face to Face With Christ, My Savior," after which he offered another earnest prayer. Marcy gave her testimony of the new life she had found in Christ that night at Evangel Home soon after Scott had disappeared. The minister read one of the letters Scott had written to Roger, and then gave a short message entitled, "To God Be the Glory."

The congretation sang "Savior, Like a Shepherd Lead Us," a song that had been sung at our wedding twenty-eight years earlier. We knew that our Savior was still leading us. The service closed with an invitation to accept Christ as Savior, or to live more for Him. A young lady walked to the front of the sanctuary in response. The pastor and I sat on the front pew to talk and pray with this teen-age girl.

When the meeting was over, numerous friends came to us offering their sympathy. We didn't know we had so many friends! Truly, it was a time of victory and triumph that had brought glory to God.

23

HE HADN'T YET BEGUN

The two letters Scott had written to Roger still lay on the shelf in Scott's old bedroom. They had been much talked about. I had wanted to mail them, but couldn't because I didn't know who "Roger" was.

A few days after the memorial service, a friend who had attended phoned me.

"I think I may know who Roger is," she announced.

"You do? Tell me, please!" I said excitedly.

The description and timing fit perfectly; he must be the one. How Scott heard of him was uncertain, although we faintly remember offering prayer for some such person after hearing a request. Most probably this lady had asked Joel to remember him in prayer, and he had shared it with our family. This was quite some time ago and we had all forgotten—that is, all but Scott, if this truly were the same lad.

Maybe now was the time to actually mail the letters! Yet I found it hard to do, just as Scott no doubt had, and I put it off for over three weeks.

Then one night after we had gone to bed, a letter from me to Roger unexpectedly began popping into my brain. In our headboard was a pencil and a pad of paper. I fumbled to reach them and then scrawled the words in the darkness, being too lazy to get up or to turn on the light. I couldn't stop until the letter was complete.

Mary Jane Warkentin

Dear Roger,
You may have heard of Scott Warkentin being lost in the mountains at Squaw Leap above Millerton Lake on April 2. It was often in the paper and on T.V. A big search went on for three weeks, until everyone was sure that Scott must have drowned in the San Joaquin River. This proved to be true when his body was found six weeks later.

We are his parents. In going through Scott's things, we found these two letters written by Scott. We know nothing else about this, and he never said anything about Roger or these letters. Scott must have spent much time composing these letter. Probably he threw away other attempts. He really did want to help! He was a sincere boy.

So I am mailing copies of the letters to you in the hope that they will be of help as Scott intended they would be.

Most sincerely and
our best wishes to you,

Mary Jane and Joel Warkentin

I laid down the pencil and determined not to let another day pass without seeing those precious letters to their destination. I was also strongly impressed with the desire to pray for Roger. I poured out my heart to God for his cordial reception of the letters, and asked that he might have a willing ear to ponder their message.

I wasn't at all prepared for what happened a few days later, however. I was playing the piano, a favorite pastime of mine. I love to try to improvise a little on the old hymns. Most are simple songs about Jesus and the abundant life He brings. I began to sing along as I played, getting louder as the words enthralled me:

Lost, But Not Forever

>Down at the cross where my Savior died,
>Down where for cleansing from sin I cried,
>There to my heart was the blood applied;
>Glory to His name.
>
>Glory to His name,
>Glory to His name,
>There to my heart was the blood applied;
>Glory to...

The doorbell was ringing!

I hurried to answer it, still in a sort of enchanted daze.

"Oh, hi there!" I said, not recognizing the tall, slim young man standing in my doorway.

"You don't know me," he said.

No, I didn't, and yet I had greeted him with such a friendly tone. There was a silent lull while I watched him reach into his back pocket for something. Perhaps he was deaf and wanted me to answer on paper. He probably wanted some money, or to sell something. Finally he got an envelope out and held it up for me to read. I took one quick glance and, why, that was my handwriting!

Immediately it all struck home, and now I was genuinely enthusiastic.

"Roger!" I cried. "You are Roger! You got my letters and you came to see me. How nice of you!"

I was not able to hold back my exuberance. The letters our recently deceased son had written—hoping to encourage this young man and win him to Christ—had been received by him. I had never expected to see him, but here he was standing by my front door.

"Please come in, and sit down," I urged.

"What's this letter mean? What's it all about? I had to come and find out more about it," Roger said as he walked into our living room and found a place in the stuffed chair by the window. I sat on the couch across the room.

"Did you read the letters from Scott?" I asked.

"I read them."

"Did you understand what Scott was saying? My son wanted to tell you that Jesus Christ could give meaning and satisfaction to your life if you took Him as your Savior and Lord."

"Did your son know me?" he asked.

"I don't think he did."

"How did he find out about me?"

"I'm not really sure. Does the message in the letters fit—I mean about your being depressed and all that?"

"It fits."

"What did you think of Scott's solution to your problems? Did it make any sense—that Jesus could help?"

"I used to go to church."

"Do you go now?"

"No."

"Why not? It might be a good idea. You know what? You ought to go to Northwest Church. It's geared for young people—just full of kids your age. I really think you'd like it, and it might help to straighten out your life the way you'd like for it to be."

"I did go to Northwest. That's the church I went to my first two years of high school."

"You did? Hey, that's great! Then you should know a lot about Jesus and the salvation He offers."

"You have other things you want to do," Roger suggested. "I'm keeping you from them." He got up from his chair.

"Oh no, there is nothing I would rather do tonight than talk with you. This is important to me; I hope it is to you, too. Why don't you stay a little longer. I'm enjoying our conversation."

He sat down again.

"I'd better not tell you this," he began.

"Go ahead—you can tell me anything."

"It might make you mad."

"That's O.K.— I won't get mad."

"Well then, do you believe in white witches?"

Lost, But Not Forever

I was surprised, not mad...but he did deserve an answer. I told him that I didn't know much about white witches, but I did believe that there was a whole world of supernatural creatures, because the Bible has much to say about them. It says there are angels who disobeyed God called "demons," who are now the bad guys of the super-natural world. The Bible speaks of principalities, spiritual wickedness in high places, and powers. Satan—also call the devil—is their leader. "Do you believe there is a devil?" I asked.

He thought a minute, then answered, "No," and went on to tell me his viewpoint. "White witches are the good ones and black witches are bad. You think this is connected with the devil, but it isn't. I only talk to white witches. That won't hurt."

"Roger, are you sure you're not asking for trouble?" I warned.

"What trouble?"

I didn't want to be talking so much about demons, which distracted us from Jesus as our subject, but I tried to be careful not to offend this young man. I was so glad he would talk with me. Although he obviously was somewhat ill at ease, he did well to talk as freely as he did to someone he had never known—especially a middle-aged woman. I appreciated it, and was anxious to chat more.

I went on to say that by "trouble" I meant that white witches can fool you. The Bible says, "Satan himself is transformed into an angel of light" (2 Corinthians 11:14). He seemed a bit surprised to hear a verse like that.

"Oh, I think it's all right," Roger said. "There's nothing wrong with parapsychology."

"Why don't you forget about all that?" I suggested. "It may start off looking right, but it is deceiving and will lead you down and destroy you. How are you feeling these days?"

"I haven't had a good day physically or mentally for two years," was his answer.

"The good years were when you were going to church," I observed. He wasn't impressed by this insight, however.

"Roger, if you want to delve into supernatural things, why don't you let Jesus come into your life? These things have been only bringing you confusion and depression. They don't do any good, but Jesus can really help you and lift you up. I have five children about your age (I included Scott) and they are all Christians. Jesus brings them fulfillment. None of them would trade the joy and peace that Jesus gives for anything you could name. I know all kinds of kids like that. Jesus forgives sins, takes away all your guilt, gives you something to live for. There's nothing like it, I'll tell you! Then, when this life is over, He takes you to heaven where you can live forever in a new, perfect body."

Roger was deep in thought. "Why did Scott die?" he wanted to know.

It was a good question. "I don't really know why," I answered softly. "God could have kept it from happening, but He didn't, so it must have been okay with Him. I don't know...I'd like to know, too...but I just have to trust God that He knows what He's doing. That's what faith is."

"Do you have a picture of him?"

"Oh sure. Excuse me a minute, and I'll get one to show you." I scurried into the bedroom and proudly re-entered with a large picture of Scott. He looked so handsome!

Roger studied his face. "No, I've never seen him. How does he know me?"

I wondered if I should say anything about the lady that had phoned me, but really I didn't know the answer to his question, and was not even positive that he was the right "Roger," so I simply answered, "Somehow he heard of you. See, you are very special to God. God must love you very much. He put into Scott's mind a strong urge to tell you how to get rid of your problems. It was hard for Scott to write those letters. He's a good writer, but he's bashful. God very much wanted him to send those letters to you." I hoped that I had said the right thing.

Roger took the envelope out of his pocket again. It looked as if he might drop it into the waste basket!

Lost, But Not Forever

"You won't throw them away, will you?" I pleaded. "Keep them, okay? Read them over again. Hang onto those letters!"

I must have shown fear on my face, for he smiled and softly answered, "I won't," and put them safely again into his back pocket. I breathed a sigh of relief.

"Let me see your hand," Roger said next. "Hold it out."

Wondering what he wanted, I did as he asked.

"No, with the palm up," he corrected me.

I turned it over, and he began to study the lines on the palm of my hand. I didn't believe in palm reading and wasn't quite sure what to do.

Finally, shrugging his shoulders, he told me, "Naw, I can't do it. I haven't learned enough yet. I will though—just give me time."

I was glad that was over, but was sorry to see him interested in fortune telling.

"Roger," I said, trying to draw him back, "have you received any other letters from Scott?" I often wondered if Scott had succeeded in mailing anything to him.

"No, only these."

Thoughtfully. and speaking carefully, I asked, "Then could it be that Scott died so the letters would reach you? He was too hesitant to get them mailed. Those are very important letters with a real message. If you do what they say, you could be saved for all eternity. If that happened, it would be worth Scott's dying."

What an impressive thought that was!

"Well, I'll have to be going," Roger said, as he walked toward the door. We had visited about an hour. "I may come back to it, but I have to go into the other some more first."

"Back to what?" I asked. "You haven't begun yet."

"What haven't I begun?"

"You haven't begun the Christian life. Going to church doesn't mean you are a Christian. Jesus said that you have to be born again."

"Well, that's a slow process—it takes a long time."

"Roger, if you should decide you want to begin a life with Christ, you can tell Him right now, and he will come into your life immediately!"

"Maybe later," was his final reply.

I looked at him, and Christ-like love welled up within me. "Come and visit anytime, and we can talk some more," I offered, walking out with him. "Is this your motorcycle?" A big, shiny red beauty waited for him in the driveway.

"Sure is!" He hopped on, and with a roar he was gone.

I did see more of Roger. I invited him a few times to the house, and he came on his motorcycle. On one occasion he showed up for a young people's party. It was obvious that he felt a bit ill at ease, but I think he was glad to have been invited.

When I finished writing up the story about his first visit to my house (for this book) I asked Roger to come and check it out. When he arrived, Marcy happened to be here too. She had accepted Christ at Evangel Home. So Roger listened to two stories that day—his own unfinished one, and Marcy's story of her new walk with Christ. Later I traveled to his home and chatted with him there.

More importantly, I continued pouring my heart out to God in prayer that he would be saved. I wanted to carry on Scott's concern for a young lad who needed Jesus desperately. Never have I prayed for anyone more earnestly or more constantly—bombarding God's throne with my request for his salvation and for the better life that I knew this would bring.

Lost, But Not Forever

24

BITTERSWEET OBEDIENCE

God brought about many blessings and a great deal of spiritual fruit from Scott's death. I personally experienced Him teaching me some important lessons in the days which followed.

One morning, as I was visiting Evangel Home, I met a young woman who looked somewhat familiar to me.

"Hi, Mary Jane," she exclaimed. "I haven't seen you for a while." She and her children had been at the Evangel Home devotional meeting the evening Marcy accepted Christ. Her name was Pat.

"How have you been?" I asked.

"Not so good," was the dismal reply. "I came here today hoping Merabelle, the superintendent, could help me. But I didn't get to even talk with her."

As we stood on the steps, she told me her problems, which were deep and complicated. I tried to offer whatever consolation I could. My words meant more to her because she knew that I, too, was having a difficult time.

"Give me your address and I'll talk with you again later," I suggested. "Perhaps you'd like to attend our ladies' Bible study and prayer group next Tuesday morning."

"Oh yes. I'd love to go with you," she answered enthusiastically.

I knew that through the difficult situations in her life, God was training Pat so that she, in turn, could help others in similar circumstances. But first, she had to win her own victories. Why was she leaving Evangel Home just as I was about to enter? I wondered about that all week. How disappointed she would have been to go home again without talking with anyone! God surely brought us together.

During that week I prepared for the Bill Glass Evangelistic Crusade. Bill is a former professional football player who is

Mary Jane Warkentin

now doing Christian work. His ministry emphasizes prison work and city-wide crusades. Joel and I felt that God wanted us to serve as counselors for the crusade, even though we were still in the midst of a personal tragedy ourselves. We had attended four weekly preparation rallies for volunteer helpers. How eagerly we looked forward to it! It would take our minds off ourselves, as well as be of service to others.

On the first day of the crusade, I was unusually busy since I had to prepare my lesson for the Bible study and prayer group that was to meet the next morning. Yet the big thing on my mind still seemed to be Pat.

"I must see Pat," something urged me. "I have to go! But how can I—I don't have time? Lord, what shall I do?"

I gave Him one moment to answer, if He would. "I'll call Molly and ask her to go visit my new friend." I quickly decided, without really considering what God's answer to my prayer might be. I had figured out the solution without His help anyway. Molly was a good friend who attended our weekly Bible class. She loved God and would probably be willing to make such a visit.

"What's new?" asked Molly, when I reached her on the phone.

"How would you like to do some missionary work?" I asked, getting right to the point. I really was in a hurry. "I know this girl..." and I went on to explain.

"Tell me where she lives and I'll run over there this afternoon."

That sounded good and I was greatly relieved. I was sure Molly would do it. Now, with that off my mind, I could put the finishing touches on tomorrow's lesson. But how slowly it seemed to come that day! Usually I was finished by that time.

About two hours later, Molly called back. "I can't catch your friend at home," she said, "I've been over there twice. I tried, but I'm sorry that I couldn't be of more help."

What a letdown! Pat needed someone, I was sure; and God wanted me to go. But the Bill Glass meeting would be starting

Lost, But Not Forever

soon, and I had just enough time to prepare supper for the family before we would have to leave.

"Well, we did our best," I told myself, attempting to dismiss it from my mind.

I didn't fuss with supper, but it was adequate. It was going to be my first night to counsel! Anticipation was running high.

Suddenly, as I was hurrying to get ready, I realized that I could no longer ignore the plain leading of the Holy Spirit.

"I can't go to the Bill Glass meeting," I said to Joel. "There'll be no peace until I go over to Pat's house."

"If that's what God wants you to do, go ahead," was his response. "We have two cars; I'll go to the meeting, and you do what you have to do." It helped so much to have an understanding husband.

My heart was light as I drove across town, knowing that I was doing the right thing!

As I drove up to an enormous apartment complex and searched for her number, I saw Pat standing outside one of the buildings. I stopped the car and rolled down the window. "How did I ever find you?" I exclaimed—really surprised. "I couldn't find any numbers on these apartments. Anyway, how would you like to go to the Bill Glass meeting? It's half over by now, but we can get in on some of it, if you'd care to."

"I sure would!" Pat liked Christian fellowship, but had so little of it. "I'd heard a lot about the crusade and wanted to go," she said, "but I had no idea how to get there without a car. I'll get the children; we can be ready in a couple minutes." Off she ran, obviously delighted. Soon she was back with her eleven-year-old son and ten-year-old daughter.

I'm sure we were the last ones to arrive, but we were able to find Joel near the front of the huge auditorium full of people, and to hear a good part of the message. He and I acted as counselors, and quickly found that the experiences we could share about Scott helped build rapport with those to whom we talked.

Pat and her children readily agreed to attend the meetings the next night. Joel went along with me to pick up the family, and

Mary Jane Warkentin

also two of their neighbor's children. When the invitation to accept Jesus was given that night, Pat, her two children, and one of their friends went forward for counseling. The children became Christians and Pat rededicated her life to the Lord. The other neighbor child was asleep by then, or she too might have joined them.

They attended on other evenings as well, and Pat has often taken part in my Bible study groups since then. Her problems seemed to fade in importance as she filled her life with more satisfying activities and more pleasant thoughts.

Surely all this was why the Holy Spirit insisted that I answer His call to visit this family, even when I was very busy.

25

CAMPING FUN

I feared one thing as we adjusted to life without Scott. Our family always loved camping, but how could we ever go on a trip again without our youngest son?

For years there were seven of us, plus all our baggage and camping equipment. One year we had three kids in diapers! But we went anyway, and that was before disposables. We always had such fun times traveling up and down California, hoping the kids wouldn't beg to go home before we arrived at our destination. It usually took about as long to pack and unpack as to go on the vacation.

Joel and the boys would pitch our tent in the most scenic spot we could find. No motels could match the decor of those surroundings! I'd begin by inflating air mattresses. This was my way of recuperating. It made me look ambitious, but really all I had to do was lie there and blow—seven mattresses, mind you.

Meals were the utmost in simplicity, eaten outdoors on a picnic table. They were "five-can", "six-can", or "seven-can" meals, warmed up on a little two-burner stove. I never could quite figure out how I had more time when we did it the hard way than when living at home.

We hiked through woods and valleys, and explored the delightful wonders of God's majestic creation. We ran and swam and laughed, and spent hours repacking an unending pile of belongings when we moved.

If there were no campfire meeting, we'd play games in the evenings, after a time of family Bible reading and prayer.

One by one the children grew older and became involved in their own interests and responsibilities, until it was just the two of us and Scott. He was the only child who had the privilege of going camping with us alone. How different it was to have elbow room for a change! We packed that last year together full of pleasant memories, just the three of us.

Now though, if we ever went again, he wouldn't be there. I didn't know how I could ever look at a campsite again.

But, one day in late summer, Joel suggested we try it. Immediately I shrank from the thought. Yet, somehow, I bravely said, "Yes." What I really dreaded was the first night—the very first lovely spot Scott could not share with us. I knew the reality of it all would hit me then. I was just sure I would see Scott under every bush and tree. I'd sense him swimming beside me in the lake, but he wouldn't be there. I'd bawl the whole time!

God must have a sense of humor. I say that reverently, because He had the most remarkable way of softening the blow.

I never shed a tear at our first campsite. It was the ugliest place you could ever find! We hunted and drove for miles the first afternoon, searching for an attractive spot. There just wasn't any! Each one looked worse than the one before.

In desperation, since it was getting late, we finally drove blindly into any old place we could find. We stepped out among the litter and dipped into the "icky" lake, only because the weather was so hot we couldn't stand it, and the shower was too smelly to use. The evening was spent starting to write this book, because there was no place to hike. We were glad Scott didn't have to be there to share the dreariness with us! Never before, or since, have we found ourselves in such a situation; or stayed in a place like that! It served its purpose, and now I like to laugh and thank God for the funny way He chose to help us.

Truly, He is an all-wise God!

Lost, But Not Forever

26

WHY?

What forms of preparation for death Scott himself received from God—if any—we cannot know. Perhaps the Lord did say to him in a still, small voice, "Will you die for me?" As his parents, we feel that he would most likely have said, "Yes."

I was looking one day through some of his old papers from the church youth group. The subject they had studied three months before he drowned was "Death." His notes included the Christian's attitude toward death, how to prepare your soul for it, and what death was like. Little did that group know what practical teaching this would prove to be. Scott's passing made a deep impression on them all. They were inspired by recalling his sincere approach to life, his closeness to God, and his knowledge of the Bible. Each one realized that he ought to take more initiative in being friendly to the quieter ones. "What a blessing," I often said, "That we were in a church among friends when all this happened."

Certain questions kept rising in my mind, however: Why did Scott die? Was Scott's death really the will of God? Did God want it that way? Surely He did not cause the tragedy, but if the Lord had chosen, I believe He could have prevented it.

Proverbs 5:21 says, "For the ways of man are before the eyes of the Lord, and He pondereth all his goings." Another verse states, "The lot is cast into the lap; but the whole disposing thereof is of the Lord" (Proverbs 16:33). So according to Scripture, God definitely has His hand in the happenings that occur to His children. There must then be a reason why God permitted Scott's death.

I wondered if it were all right for me to even think of "why." As I pondered this, I recalled Jesus' words on the cross—He asked, "Why?" when He said, "My God, my God, why hast Thou forsaken Me?" So I decided that it was all right for me also to ask, but that I should not question His wisdom in allowing what is best.

Why, then, should God have let such a thing happen without intervening? Very likely it was a combination of reasons. One I thought of may be expressed in the verse, "The fining pot is for silver and the furnace for gold: but the Lord trieth the hearts" (Proverbs 17:3). It certainly has been a refining process for Joel and our children and me, and for many others as well.

We don't like to admit it, but the Bible teaches that there is a purpose in suffering. It all seems so useless and wasteful to us, but God knows better. We see the underside of the "embroidery" of life—full of knots and tangled with ugly threads. But God has the view from above! He sees the finished product, which is actually beautiful and orderly. It takes an awful lot of faith to see it His way, if we ever do. Satan is continually trying to get us down, thinking all the time that he is fighting against God. Yet our almighty and wise God has a way of turning it around—using that very thing for good, instead of the evil the devil intended. It is said that suffering will make us bitter, or it will make us better. The choice is completely up to us!

Or perhaps this passage could be an answer as to why Scott had to leave this earth when he did: "Merciful men are taken away, none considering that the righteous is taken away from the evil to come" (Isaiah 57:1). Maybe God wished to spare Scott from future evils which might befall him.

Possibly it all happened so this book could be written and someone encouraged by it. He may have been born for this reason. Is that why I wanted a fifth child so much? If you are inspired in some way to live closer to Jesus, then my "life verse" will be realized. Long ago I decided on this verse as my purpose in living: "That your rejoicing may be more abundant in Jesus Christ" (Philippians 1:26). My life's prayer is that the Lord will use me to help increase the rejoicing of others. Scott is having a part in this.

Quite a ministry has already developed for me in giving speeches on Scott's disappearance and how God helped us through it. The speaking engagements have included Bible study groups, missionary societies, Christian Women's Club luncheons, a Sunday School class, and even dinner parties. These talks have proven a blessing to me as well as to others. Sometimes Marcy tags along to give her testimony.

One lady wrote afterward, "I always wanted to meet you; and as God would have it, I was able to do so at a very much needed time—right before Bob's death. Wasn't God wonderful in allowing you to speak there that day? Wow! What an impact your sharing had on me and Mom. It was one of the factors leading to my acceptance of Bob's death. That was the most heart-breaking day of my life, but it hasn't broken my spirit or caused my faith to falter. I thank the Lord for you." Can you imagine how happy this made me feel to know that God had chosen to use me as a channel for Him to help her?

Another woman's husband was in a wreck the day after I had shared God's blessings. It was a very foggy day, and when she heard on the radio of a multiple car accident in the area, she began to panic. Then things she had heard at the talk came to her mind, including some pertinent Bible verses. She was able to continue through the day with an unusual calmness and peace of mind. His car was demolished in that accident, but he came through all right.

Why do bad things happen to good people? Because others in similar difficulties need an experienced Christian to help them along the way. If everything is rosy for us, we will never be trusted as a worthy comforter. We need to sit where they sit, so we and they both know that we do understand.

27

MORE AND MORE

As Christmas approached, lists of "What I Want for Christmas" began to be taped to the bedroom doors in our home, even from the boys who had moved away from home.

Somehow I couldn't get into the spirit of things. I left my door blank. I didn't care what I received for Christmas, and I certainly wasn't in the mood to shop for anyone else. I didn't even want a tree. I thought it would be better if we skipped the holidays altogether.

But one day, as I was perusing through some large cardboard boxes in Scott's old bedroom, my eyes just about popped out of my head when I saw a sheet of paper on top of everything else in one of the boxes. "Dear Roger," it began. As I quickly scanned the page, I knew that it was another letter from Scott to Roger—a third one! When I picked it up, to my amazement underneath was a <u>fourth</u> letter to Roger. Pulling the large box down from the shelf, I flipped through other pages, and realized that what I had discovered was a box absolutely full of unmailed letters and papers. I was completely astounded and thrilled! Scott had written them all.

I ran to the telephone immediately and called my daughter.

"Renetta!" I shouted in jubilation when she answered the phone. Then I began to laugh and cry at the same time.

"What's the matter, Mom?" Renetta queried with concern. She couldn't quite figure out if something good or something bad had happened. I tried to answer, but suddenly burst into tears instead.

As soon as I was able to control my voice, I tried to set her at ease. "No, it's something good, Renetta—I'm happy."

"Well, tell me!" my daughter demanded.

"I found a whole box of 'Roger letters,'" I blurted out.

"You what? 'Roger letters'? That Scott wrote?"

Lost, But Not Forever

"Yes." Tears of joy were still streaming down my face. "I don't know why I never noticed these papers before, Renetta."

"Where did you find them?"

"In a big cardboard box in Scott's room. When I realized what was in there, I didn't want to look at them all alone, so I called you. I've barely had a glimpse myself, Renetta—there are dozens of letters in there. I just can't believe it."

We began going through them together. Some were in pencil, some in ink, some written long-hand, and others he had printed. Many began the same way, then every one took a little different turn—each clearly with the same purpose: to encourage Roger to turn to Jesus for the salvation of his soul and a happier and more wholesome life than he had ever known.

"Look!" I exclaimed in surprise, "here's one to Johnny...one more to Johnny! More!" Johnny lived across the street and had been a friend of Ralph's. I turned a few sheets and found letters to Mrs. Todd. I burst into a smile of pure pleasure. Mrs. Todd? Why did Scott write to Mrs. Todd? She was an older lady and he didn't even know her. Or did he? Everyone in our neighborhood was acquainted with the Todd Lapidary Shop down the street. She and her husband had been interested in rocks for years, and we always wondered if her living room was filled with beautiful polished rocks. We all knew <u>about</u> her, but none of us had ever met her. Or so I thought.

I recalled a Halloween when our children were much younger and were out trick-or-treating. I lingered behind in the darkness. The Todds' front door had slowly opened in answer to the knock of our cute little "spooks." There was only a lighted reflection of a life-sized skeleton being flashed on and off a screen just inside the house! Our children did not meet Mrs. Todd that right. They took one scary glance at that big lighted skeleton and they scurried off as fast as they could, before she had a chance to offer them any treats. But would that inspire Scott to write a letter like this to Mrs. Todd?

Mary Jane Warkentin

I kept looking in the box and Renetta listened intently. "More to Roger...another to Johnny...here's a letter to the Fujimoto family."

I really did believe that I might only be dreaming, because I have sometimes experienced wondering during a dream if I was awake or dreaming. I never knew for sure until I woke up. But no, this was positively real! And I liked what I saw! I read scattered portions of the letters out loud to my daughter while we laughed and cried together.

"I wish you could be here, Renetta, but I'll talk with you later." The rest of the morning I spent going through the box in more detail to see what else it might contain.

As I continued investigating, I found another surprise.

"What is this?" I asked myself. It wasn't a letter. Softly—as if in awe—I said, "Why this is a prayer written by Scott."

> Oh Jesus, I ask you to forgive me. I have not sought you. Thank you. You are good. Jesus, speak to Roger through me. I ask how I will serve you, then I can't tell others of you. Help me to obey you. Glory be to the Lord! Praise the Lord, dear Lord, for forgiveness.

There were other prayers also, and notes on Scripture passages. One was a summary of Romans 12: "We should let God control our lives; we should do all we can with our abilities God has given us; we should really love others; we should stand on the side of good! Work for the Lord enthusiastically; don't think you know it all; let God punish people instead of you...work for Him, live for Him, no MATTER WHAT THE CIRCUMSTANCES—be not a Christian in vain."

So good! So inspiring! Yet he struggled so. He had wanted to get these letters to people for whom he had a concerned interest, yet all he could do was sit at home and write more letters.

Then there were old left-over toys at the very bottom of the box.

Lost, But Not Forever

It was the most wonderful Christmas present ever!

I had found a total of sixty-eight letters—forty-two of them directed to Roger—and many prayers and notes he had made on Bible passages.

God must have lifted my blindness so that I could find those letters just in time for a happy Christmas. It really seemed as if Scott were with us. And in a new way he was. I am sure I must have looked in that box before, because I had searched through Scott's papers for Roger's address. He had stated in his first letter that he had "already addressed and stamped an envelope" to Roger, but it hadn't been mailed. I had wanted to find that envelope. I did not find it, but one letter in this new group included Roger's last name, so at last I was certain that I had found the right person. The youth who had visited me was without a doubt the one Scott had intended to reach. Now the papers were so obvious and easily seen, that it seemed impossible to have missed them before.

Scott had not been "a Christian in vain." He had poured out his heart on paper, and now we felt that he was opening it up to us and letting us understand him in a way that he never did when he was with us. We were grateful.

Truly, "we know that all things work together for good to them that love God, to them who are the called according to his purpose" (Romans 8:28).

28

HOPELESS

"What should I do with all these writings of Scott's?" I wondered. I felt responsible for using them wisely for something more than my own consolation.

"I'll deliver them myself!"

Mrs. Todd and the Fujimoto family soon each received a visit from me, along with one or two of the best letters from Scott. Johnny was in the Navy, so I wrote him a nice letter and enclosed the letters. Since forty-two of them were addressed to Roger, I began mailing his one by one, often enclosing a friendly note.

Roger phoned me after receiving ten of them.

"Do you still have more letters from Scott to send me?" he asked.

"Yes."

"Then I want to ask you not to send any more of them."

"Why?" I said rather stunned! I didn't like his attitude.

"They don't do me any good. I can read them, but I don't want you to send them anymore."

"Oh Roger, that breaks my heart," I admitted. "Scott wrote those letters for you, and I really like sending them to you." It was a real let-down.

"You'll get over it," he assured me.

"I know, but why don't I mail them all at once?" I suggested hopefully.

"No."

"O.K. then. How are you doing?"

"No good."

I was genuinely sorry to hear that. "You could have a better life. You know that, don't you?"

"I don't care about anything anymore. I'm going to be seeing God sooner than I thought."

Lost, But Not Forever

That was a shocking statement! Was he planning to kill himself soon? I had to say the right thing.

"Roger, I want you to know that I really care—I'm concerned about what happens to you."

"You wouldn't be if you knew me. I can't be honest with anyone. Maybe I should fib more and not tell people things."

"No," I replied. "I like it better when people are honest and say it like it really is. I don't care for all this cover-up stuff. It doesn't matter what you say or do, I'm still going to stick by you. I'm really glad you called, because I've wanted to talk more with you. What you say isn't going to shock me—I'm used to that." I braced myself to be sure that it wouldn't.

I had to get to the point. "I just don't want you going to hell, Roger!"

I didn't mean to say that he was a bad person. He was as good as any of the rest of us. But I knew that none of us are good enough. Just as a baby can't come into the world unless he is born, so we can't get into heaven until we are born again. Every one of us needs to make a new spiritual beginning before he is ready to face death. The Bible says, "Except a man be born of water and of the spirit, he cannot enter into the kingdom of God" (John 3:5). We all have to turn ourselves over to Jesus and let Him make us new. Roger had not yet done this.

"What do you think about Jesus? Do you think He is alive now?" I asked sincerely, trying to find something to build on.

"Maybe He is and maybe He isn't."

"Do you think He rose from the dead?"

"I don't know if He did or not, but I'll be real mad at God if I find out there's no heaven! I spent all my life thinking about it and I'll sure hate God for not having a heaven.."

I felt like saying, "Why should you care since you're not preparing for it anyway?"

But I hesitated a moment before replying. "God wants you to be there with Him when the proper time comes. He has all kinds of good things for you. It's up to you if you want them or not. You know, it's amazing how God can give you peace. Even though you say this world is a mess, you can have your own inner security. The Bible calls it 'the peace that passeth understanding.'"

Roger was silent.

"Have you been to see Bufe yet?" Bufe was the pastor of Northwest Church, which Roger used to attend. Bufe had already told me that he had talked with Roger very recently.

"That guy doesn't do anybody any good," Roger declared. "He's no help."

"What can I do to help you?"

"Just stop sending the letters."

"O.K., no more letters, but we're praying for you."

"It doesn't do any good."

"There's a lot of power in prayer."

"God doesn't have much power."

"He doesn't?" I exclaimed, raising my voice. "He made all the world and the universe! It takes a lot of power to do that!"

My heart went out to him. "You're missing out on all the good things God wants to give you. He's got a great life for you if you'll just take it. I know lots of people—I don't mean just a few, but many, many people—who were really down and their lives all mixed up, and they turned to God and it was so much better. They just said, 'I wish I had done that long ago.'"

Roger had it all figured out—"If I do that," he concluded, "you know what it'll mean? I'll have to change my whole lifestyle, get all new friends, and a completely new environment."

I thought about that a minute. "You're exactly right. It would mean a good bit of that. But you couldn't do all that changing by yourself. That's impossible for anyone to do. You'd need to tell God, 'Here I am—You take over and run my life.' You'd need to turn it over to Him and the two of you together could do whatever changing is needed."

I waited a moment or two for this to sink in, then continued with an important question, "Have you rejected Christ, then?" Perhaps I should have turned it around and asked if he would

Lost, But Not Forever

receive Christ, but he didn't seem ready for that, or I wasn't brave enough.

He paused. "You might say I have; yes, lots of times I do reject Him. Yes, I've rejected Christ."

"Well, there may be a time when you'll want to come to Him. Then you can, if you haven't rejected Him too much."

"Don't you think it's too late for that now?" Roger said.

"Too late? Why?"

"I'm almost twenty years old. I ought to be getting married now."

"No," I laughed, "you're not a bit too old."

But he thought otherwise. "In ten years I'll be thirty. And in ten more years, I'll be forty years old."

Oh, the perspective of youth, I thought. Then I told him, "Even forty still seems young to me. But twenty? That's a very good time to accept Christ. I don't know of a better age."

Another awkward pause.

Then he said, "If Scott had something to say to me, how come he didn't come to me and say it? Don't you think he could have at least mailed those things to me then? It's kind of late to be hearing from him now after he's dead."

"You're right, Roger," I answered. "He should have. But we don't all do what we should do. From other things Scott wrote I found that he felt very bad because he wasn't obeying God. He was very bashful. He may not sound shy in the letters, but he was. He had a difficult time confronting people. He felt so bad about it! Scott wrote that he couldn't call God 'Lord' because he'd disobeyed Him. So I'm trying to carry on his work. I'm not perfect, either. If you look to Christians, you can find lots of things wrong. We are sinners too. But most true Christians are trying to do right, and they want to be better. You can only look to God for someone perfect."

To that Roger said, "Christians are just like rich people. They look down on others who don't have what they do."

"Yes." His analogy was very good. "I believe you're right. Christians do have a lot of good things. And they are always

Mary Jane Warkentin

wishing it on others. They are much like rich people." I asked him if he liked talking about these things.

"Yeah, except that being honest shows things up and I lose friends that way. Except that I really don't have any friends that like me anyway."

"I'll always like you," I responded quickly, "no matter what. I'll always be concerned about you."

"I believe that's the truth."

"So you don't want any more letters? There are forty-two of them. I figured it might take just that many for you to decide to take Jesus as your Savior. I really thought something great would happen on number forty-two."

"No, there's no hope for me. I'm not afraid of anything."

"You're not afraid to meet God the way you are?"

"Nope, I'm not scared of Him—I'll get Him!" Roger seemed to be very sure of that.

"O.K. then, thanks a million for calling and for coming over those times. I really appreciated it."

We said our goodbyes, and I felt that we'd had a good talk. But I was very uneasy about his statement that he would be seeing God sooner than he expected. It all seemed so hopeless and had been for such a long time. Was this a suicide warning? Should I do something about it? What could I do? No one else was at home for me to consult, so it was all up to me. I remembered that a person should take such comments seriously. Not knowing what to do, I did nothing, but busied myself again with household chores.

A half hour later I heard the eerie screech of a siren. An ambulance tore down the busy street.

I melted!

29

NOTHING SPECIAL

Roger did not kill himself that day.

I stopped mailing the letters, but his name was often whispered in prayer. He was not forgotten.

Perhaps a year later, a friend and I happened to be driving near Roger's home. I had an urge to drop in.

He still lived there, and answered the door when I knocked. Right away I noticed that Roger looked different. His expression had a peaceful look—a serenity. He invited us in and offered refreshments.

"By the way," he mentioned casually after we were settled, "have I ever told you that I have become a Christian?"

"No, Roger, you never told us that, but I knew something had happened the moment you opened the door. Tell us, how did this come about?"

"Nothing special. I just asked Jesus to come into my heart one day."

"Did you go forward in a church service, or did anyone talk with you about it?"

"No, nothing like that. I wanted to do it, so I did—just by myself at home."

"Are you glad?"

"I sure am. Now I read the Bible and am learning more about the Christian life."

No one on earth knows how much this meant to me!

We had a little time of Bible study right there. "I'm so happy for you," I said. "It won't always be easy, but now you have Someone to help you all along the way."

It hasn't been easy for Roger, but the last I heard he was still hanging in there. He has become a new person. "Therefore if any man be in Christ, he is a new creature: old things are passed away; and behold, all things are become new" (2 Corinthians 5:17).

Roger turned from reading palms to reading Psalms! Now he knows how great and powerful God is. He no longer rejects Christ, but has come into a personal experience of the Son of God as his Savior, Lord, and constant companion. He is "saved": that is, Roger has been forgiven of all his past sins, is given daily power to overcome present temptations, and is promised a future free from condemnation. And he has the "peace of God which passeth all understanding" (Philippians 4:7). Roger also now knows the power of prayer and intercedes for the needs of others. He is rich! Romans 9:23 says. "And that he might make known the riches of his glory on the vessels of mercy."

At last Roger has hope. His present state can be expressed this way: "Blessed be the God and Father of our Lord Jesus Christ, which according to his abundant mercy hath begotten us again unto a lively hope by the resurrection of Jesus Christ from the dead, to an inheritance incorruptible, and undefiled, and that fadeth not away, reserved in heaven for you" (I Peter 1:3-4).

Scott and the angels are probably rejoicing over Roger's Christian walk, and they will happily greet him with open arms when his turn comes to enter heaven.

One of these days I hope to get the other thirty-two letters to him. Roger told me that he would like to read them now.

EPILOGUE

Scott is still a part of our family. When people ask, "How many children do you have?" I say, "Five, but one of them is in heaven." Scott may have left the earthly body in which he used to reside, and we no longer hear from him, but he is actually more alive now than he has ever been. He was <u>lost, but not forever</u>. He lives on in heaven! Here is a song which a friend wrote and sang to us:

> Rejoice, rejoice—thy son has been found!
> Thy precious, loving son's been found.
> Rejoice, rejoice—thy son has been found.
> He's in heaven with our Lord.
> He walks with him...talks with him.
> Watches over and cares for him.
> He laughs with him throughout each day;
> He's in heaven with our Lord!

We don't believe that Scott went to heaven as a reward for being good, since the Bible says, "For by grace are ye saved through faith; and that not of yourselves: it is the gift of God: not of works lest any man should boast" (Ephesians 2:8,9). Scott had faith in the finished work of Christ on the cross. "Jesus paid it all," says the song. He had trusted Jesus as his Savior from sin and hell, and that is why we believe he was granted entrance into God's presence.

God has certainly worked in my life. I thought of the night when He gave me assurance, "Don't worry, it's all in my hands." He could have said instead, "Don't worry, Scott's with me." But He didn't tell me that. He must have wanted to stretch my faith by giving me confidence in Him, but not answers. I had to be completely dependent upon His loving wisdom, and in doing so I have grown spiritually.

Mary Jane Warkentin

One day I was contemplating what all these experiences had done for me and how I had become richer. Although I have lost the pleasure of being with my much-loved son, and certainly would never have chosen this for myself, still I have grown in many valuable ways:

* Heaven seems so close now. I think more about it, and am more and more eagerly awaiting the experience of going there. Along with this, there is a great lessening of the fear of death. There is more to be feared in life than in death.

* I realize that it is possible to make it through difficult situations, because God gives the additional grace necessary to cover my inabilities if I look to Him.

* It is now proven that what I believe and what the Bible teaches is true, and can pass the test of life in the real world.

* I have found a wide-open opportunity for witnessing—by sharing my everyday experiences, and how God is working through them.

* Although there may be some hypocrites in the church and elsewhere, I saw much genuine Christian love in action—so much that it was completely overwhelming.

* The Warkentin family has been bound together in a new closeness.

Mary Jane and Joel gave flowers for the church five years after Scott's disappearance.

* My bothersome inferiority complex blew out the window (almost, at least). After hearing so many heart-felt "we love you"s from so many sources and seeing so much tangible evidence of love, I have begun to accept myself as a person who can be, and is, loved. It feels so good!

* I discovered that it is possible to live solely by faith—to trust when I don't understand.

* At least for a while, I thought I had settled on a hair-do that I felt looked right, after seeing myself twice on television.

God is also continuing to work in Marcy's life. She and I began weekly times of fellowship, and soon other new Christians from Evangel Home gathered with us each Saturday morning for

Mary Jane Warkentin

intensive Bible study and prayer. Marcy has grown in the Lord. But it has not taken place without trials and setbacks. She wants to please Jesus, her Savior. And she states frankly, "Scott had to die so I could be saved."

When Marcy joined a church, she gave this testimony of what Jesus meant to her: "Jesus, You are the only man in all the world—both heaven and earth—that I can really trust. I've come to know You as my personal Savior. You took away the crutch that I had been using all my life—that nobody loves me. You loved me so much that You took my place on that awful cross. You have freed my heart and soul to enable me to express genuine love, and put me in a place I needed to be all my life—a place where people can love me, and I them. You are enabling me to be strong in eliminating all the garbage from my life. I am trying to witness to You in every thought, word, and deed; and to stand up to the devil when he draws too near, and to cast him out of my heart and mind." It's a daily battle, and Marcy does not attain her high goal all the time. But she is on the way and going in the right direction.

The other young lady—the one who responded to the invitation at the memorial service—has consistently attended another Sunday School and church. Donald was her teacher for some time. She is progressing spiritually and, also, is studying to be a doctor.

As to the Bill Glass Crusade, I have seen God's mighty hand in the follow-up work. Each counselor was assigned to meet informally several times with one of those who had come forward during the invitations. "You may be surprised at how appropriately the two of you will be matched by God," we had been told in the preparation rally. It was true! Joel was appointed to follow up with another school teacher, and I was given the name of a mother. When I phoned her, I found that this lady's son had drowned just the day before Scott's drowning.

Joel and I are grateful that most of our children—Wayne, Renetta, and Donald—seem to have made it through Scott's passing without mishap. Ralph had a more difficult time. However, it did tend to deepen all of their spiritual lives.

Ralph had much soul-searching to do. Even before Scott's death he was having trouble walking the "narrow way." His younger brother and best friend leaving this earth was a real jolt for him. The Holy Spirit began speaking to his heart, and after awhile he dedicated his life anew to the Lord at a Christian concert. This brought gladness into his life, and more stability.

Later a friend of Ralph's who had not seen him for some time, asked. "Have you started going to the bars yet?"

"No, not me," Ralph answered with conviction, "I have no interest in anything like that. I've come clean—cleaned up clear through, and Christ now is the center of my life." She gazed in amazement. "If anyone says something nice about me now," Ralph declares, "I usually let them know why I'm that way. It's because Jesus is in my life."

He dropped his pin-striping job and traveled on his own to the Gilbert Islands—a remote spot in the Pacific—and became a short-term missionary, helping build a thatched-roof church and teaching in its school.

Our three sons now – Donald, Wayne, and Ralph.

Renetta's children twenty years later – Tiffany, Matthew, and Carolyn – our only grandchildren. Carolyn has graduated from beauty college and has begun her career as a hairdresser.

Renetta's family now.
Front row – Tiffany and Renetta.
Center - her husband, Rick.
Back row - Carolyn, Matthew, and Sarah (Matthew's wife).

Lost, But Not Forever

However, something cracked—a mental illness, schizophrenia, has overtaken Ralph. This provides another challenge for our family to trust when we don't understand. He came back to the States and is doing very well. He is happy living in his own apartment (but visiting his parents often.) He has three ministries 1.) prayer, 2.) memorizing and quoting Bible verses, and 3.) giving out Christian tracks. He is even a deacon in his church! About Scott, he admits, "it boggles my mind. I try not to think about it anymore, but it keeps coming up. But I'm sure glad we had him for fifteen years, aren't you, Mom?"

"Absolutely!" I said without hesitation.

The oldest boy, Wayne, thinks back on the many hours he spent trampling around—searching for his brother. It was utterly miserable, and he suffered great financial troubles after taking so much time off work. But he survived. Life has sent many difficulties his way, but his desire still is to get into full-time Christian work.

Our son Donald, who ran with the dogs, finally completed his doctor's degree in the study of insects, and is working for the federal department of agriculture seeking to control pests which prey on our crops. He still likes to sing and often thinks of the time when his 500-voice choir was singing exultantly "When We All Get To Heaven." It was very likely that his brother was just then spending his very first moments in that heavenly home!

Through the long, grueling experiences, Joel has also arrived at a place of deeper trust in the Lord. One Bible passage has become expecially meaningful to him, "I want you to trust me in your times of trouble, so I can rescue you, and you can give me glory" (Psalm 50:15 THE LIVING BIBLE). He also came across this helpful prayer: "Lord, help me not to dread what might happen, not to worry about what could happen, but to accept what does happen, because You care for me."

During the many hours of searching and waiting, the reality of Joel's faith in God was tested. Was trust in the Lord really the type of lifestyle to follow? He became more than ever convinced that it was. Joel's renewed decision was "to God be the glory." My husband often reflected on the ordeal, and repeatedly received this message: Joel, this needed to be, it was best that it be this way, and it's the best outcome. Along with this came a peace— a settled feeling.

I have been asked if I had any premonition of impending doom. Only this: about a week before Scott vanished the thought came to me, "What if you would have to lose one of your sons—which one would it be?"

"I don't want to lose any of my sons," I declared.

"But if you had to, which would you choose?"

"I love each one of them," I insisted. "I don't want to lose any one of my sons!"

The thought persisted, and it seemed that there was a strong urgency for me to name a son. I couldn't get out of it. I had to...so finally I said, "Scott." He was the youngest, thus having the farthest to go in his preparation for life.

I told this to my brother, Walter, after the drowning and asked him if he thought it was all nonsense.

His reply was, "How old were you then?"

"Fifty- four."

"Has anything similar to this ever happened to you before?"

"No."

"And you have four sons," he said thoughtfully. "It is quite amazing that out of fifty-four years and four sons you should name the one that was about to be 'lost' just before it actually happened." Strangly enough, Wayne also had a strikingly similar experience about the same time without knowing anything about mine.

If these incidents have significance, then maybe Joel's experience does too. All through our married life Joel never would accept the thought that he could live to be an old man. He considered his thirties to be well into middle age, and thought of himself as an old man in his forties and fifties, although he actually held his age extremely well, and most people thought he was younger than he was. Also he was very healthy. I could never quite understand this way of thinking, and I must admit it

Lost, But Not Forever

irritated me somewhat, since I always felt young at heart whatever my age or physical condition, and I thought he should too.

One day, he made an attention-getting statement: "I may as well tell you this now, since there's no longer need for concern. I never wanted to worry you.."

"Wow! What?" I exclaimed.

"Sit down, and I'll tell you."

I sat.

"When I was young," he began, "about Scott's age of fifteen, a very forceful thought made its way into my mind. It was so intense that I could never forget it in all these years. It was that death would come at fifty-five. I have always thought I would die at that age. But now I've had my fifty-sixth birthday and it didn't happen. So I may live to be an old man yet!

I reflected on what my husband said. It was not like such a down-to-earth-common-sense person as he to make such a statement. But as I thought about it, I realized that it was true that death <u>did</u> come to him at fifty-five—not his death, but Scott's. It was just two days after Joel had finished his fifty-fifth year that Scott left this earth! Was Scott's life destined to be just that long? If so, then in that time he was to accomplish his life's work. I believe he did. And the effects of his short life are still going on, as you can see from the events related in this book.

Time has passed quickly for us. Joel and I have finally reached old age. We are now 79 and 78 years old and just celebrated our 51st wedding aniversary. What a gala party our children gave us for our 50th! They went all out to make it a happy occasion. We keep busy now with many volunteer Christian ministries which still includes Bible studies at Evangel Home.

Mary Jane Warkentin

Mary Jane and Joel celebrate their 50th wedding anniversary

Renetta's husband, Rick, gave his best efforts on Scott's behalf, clocking up many dreary hours battling that mountaious terrain. He is glad he did, and we are so grateful for his dedication to the family. Now he and Renetta are maintaining a strong Christian home for their seven-year-old Tiffany. Matthew and his wife, Sarah, are on their own as well as Matthew's younger sister, Carolyn. Time certainly does fly by! No, Matthew does not remember Scott, but he sure has heard a lot about him.

Renetta completed her college degree and is now a registered dietician. Her husband, Rick, is director of maintenance and operation in the mountain school district.

I used to tell God, "If you have some lesson You want me to learn, please don't make me go through something hard in order to teach it to me. Just tell me what Your desires are, and I will do my very best to please You. I love You, God, and I want to live for You, and I don't need discipline to make me do it."

But God knew better. There are some things of great value that can only be attained by undergoing difficult circumstances.

I have no corner on God—He can bring you through, also. I hope no one will say, "But she is such a strong person." My

Lost, But Not Forever

answer to that is an emphatic, "No, not at all! I am weak in so many ways. If you see strength, it is not mine, but is given to me by God. If there is anything I want to say, it is this: God will do the same for you when you need it! He will give you immeasurable strength to endure, if you will but let Him. He is all-powerful, and He wants to turn the hard things of your life into stepping stones. You can go on, with your hand in His. See beyond your little world, and look at things from the viewpoint of all eternity!"

"Be strong and of a good courage," the Bible says, "fear not, nor be afraid of them: for the Lord thy God, he it is that doth go with thee; he will not fail thee, nor forsake thee" (Deuteronomy 31:6).

Scott doesn't need our pity. Why, he is living in a mansion! If he were asked to return, there is no doubt that he would rather stay where he is.

His interests and evaluation of himself when he was in junior high are expressed in his "self-profile" which I found among his papers. (See page 182).

Scott didn't know how to spell "reputation" then, but he doesn't need to study any more now, because he knows everything! He had been named, "boy most likely to succeed" by his junior high graduating class because of his intellect, but he never told us about that. We found out about it after he was gone. He had listed "knowledge" as his "gift" on a church questionaire on talents. But now, as the Bible says, "then shall I know even as also I am known" (1 Corinthians 13:12). Why, he can no doubt speak Spanish fluently now. How happy he must be to <u>know</u> it <u>all!</u>

He no longer needs any of the fun things he enjoyed on earth, for "in thy presence is fullness of joy; at thy right hand there are pleasures forevermore" (Psalm 16:11).

Scott is with Jesus, whom he loves! He can't come back to us, but we can go to him someday. And we will be together much longer than we are now separated—for all eternity.

Self-profile

My name is **Scott Warkentin**. This is what it means to me: —

My present interests in life are **baseball, and the history and geography of the world. I like to look at maps.** Teach when am gr. up.

In the future I might be interested in **Teaching.**

Things I like about myself (what I am or can do) **I can play baseball fairly well, I know a lot about baseball, history, and geography. I am interested in many things and I am smart.**

Things I would like to improve in myself: **People like me better, To have a better repitition.**

These are the people I turn to most often for help: **My brother and my mother.**

My greatest failure is **not having a good repitition, much shyness**

Two things I can do well are **baseball and quiz questions.**

The one question I would most like to have answered is —

One dream I have for the future is **to have a better repitition and to have a better relationship with God.**

The thing I most need from my friends is **to be kinder to me.**

Lost, But Not Forever

What is Scott doing now? I wanted to know too, so I searched the Bible for an answer. Two things are sure:

First, he is praising God! Scott always did like music, even though he was not very good at it. He faithfully took four years of violin lessons at school. My how vibrantly he could use that violin bow! But it was all out of tune, and he couldn't even seem to finish a song the same time as the other players. His teacher suggested that he quit because he never seemed to improve. But he wouldn't give up. It was the same way when he sang. But now what a voice he must have with which to praise his heavenly father!

Second, he is serving God. I am sure of that because the Scripture says, "his servants shall serve him" (Revelation 22:3). The Lord must have some wonderful plan that we know nothing about. Whatever it is, His servants in heaven must be in the midst of it. Here we serve so hesitantly—so feebly. We are afraid of what people will think. We don't want to offend. Scott had such a hard time getting the letters written to Roger, and then he could never mail them. He also wanted to witness about Christ to his classmates, but he just couldn't do that either. But now? Now he serves God with no inhibitions! Nothing holds him back. He has perfect freedom. What a satisfaction that must bring to someone who loves to serve his Savior! Perhaps the service of those in heaven has something to do with us here on this earth! Surely there is nothing more dear to God's heart than the people He created for His own pleasure. Could Scott possibly be having a part in influencing people or circumstances to help answer prayers? He may still be more a part of his family's lives than we realize. It's something to think about.

We really don't know. There is much about which to speculate. The Warkentin family wonders many things, but our youngest member has all the answers!

Mary Jane Warkentin

> HE WILL SWALLOW UP
> DEATH IN VICTORY
> AND THE LORD GOD
> WILL WIPE
> AWAY TEARS FROM ALL FACES.
>
> (Isaiah 25:8)

Mary Jane Warkentin would be glad to hear from you. She can be reached at 2320 West Carmen Avenue, FRESNO CA 93728 or by phone at (559) 266-8837.